DAILY
MOTIVATION

*365 Messages to Inspire
You at Work and in Life*

NIDO R. QUBEIN

Editing by: Alice Patenaude

Photo Credits
Cover: front, hakkiarslan/Getty Images

Published by Simple Truths, an imprint of Sourcebooks, Inc.
P.O. Box 4410, Naperville, Illinois 60567–4410
(630) 961–3900
Fax: (630) 961–2168
www.sourcebooks.com

Printed and bound in China.
QL 10 9 8 7 6 5 4 3 2 1

MOTIVATION BY THE MONTH

INTRODUCTION

Dear Readers,

U se this book as a guide to start conversations with friends, family, even strangers. Or use it to ignite change within yourself.

Read it, put it down, and read it again. Let it influence your heart and impact your soul.

In the student seminars I teach at High Point University, I often remind the students of one of my favorite quotes. It's from writer Mark Twain.

"The two most important days in your life are the day you are born and the day you discover why."

If you want to improve your life, you have to examine what you believe. You have to stand for something or you will fall for anything, and there is no such thing as unrealistic dreams—only unrealistic time lines.

We live in a transformative time, and the future is not for the fainthearted. It belongs to the brave. So, be brave.

Transform yourself, make your dreams happen, and pursue your own goals that will make your world a better place.

You can do it. Create your own powerful current that can sweep you toward unexpected triumphs. The only person stopping you is you. Your future is all yours.

So good luck. Godspeed. May this book be the wind that helps you sail toward a brighter horizon—and toward a better you.

Nido R. Qubein
President
High Point University
nqubein@highpoint.edu

JANUARY

IT BEGINS TODAY

JANUARY 1

A new year is all about where you have been, where you are **now**, where you want to **go**. Present circumstances don't determine where you go. They merely determine where you start.

Writer Mark Twain called New Year's a "harmless annual institution." And **yes**, there is nothing extraordinary about the date January 1. But there is something extraordinary about YOU! When God gave you life, He intended for you to be extraordinary.

Imagine today is the first day of a blank 365-page book. Write something memorable. Be courageous, visualize where you want to go and who you want to **be**, and believe in yourself.

You can make it happen. But don't fear mistakes.

"If you are making mistakes, then you are making new things, trying new things, learning, living, pushing yourself, changing yourself, changing your world. You're doing things you've never done before, and more importantly, you're doing something," said writer Neil Gaiman.

Write a resolution on your heart that theologian Jonathan Edwards made more than two centuries ago: "Resolution One: I will live for God. Resolution Two: If no one else does, I still will."

Execute with faithful courage. The Time Is Now. The Person Is You. Make this the best year yet.

FIND YOUR RIGHT ROAD

JANUARY 2

Happiness and fulfillment are two totally different things.

Some people try to use money, good looks, or good health to achieve happiness. They shouldn't. You can lose money, and you can lose your good looks and good health as you age or through a careless lifestyle.

Fulfillment, though, comes from a life well lived—one devoted to making the world a better place. When you focus on improving the world, you become a better person, one filled with a great sense of gratification.

When the final books are balanced, our reward isn't assured by the amount of money we've made, the size of the estate we've amassed, or the prestigious connections we've cultivated. It's the people we have helped, the legacy we have left, the stewardship we are invested in, the philanthropy we have displayed, and the seeds we have planted in the lives of others.

When those seeds germinate and grow, others can—in a significantly wonderful way—go out and do something worthwhile in their own lives.

Ask yourself this question: If I were to die tomorrow, what would I most regret not having done?

Face it: You're not likely to die tomorrow. What's keeping you from doing the thing you would most regret not doing?

Do it, and you will be on the road to fulfillment.

GOD'S BREATH

JANUARY 3

M ost of the limitations that keep us from realizing our full potential are artificial. They are imposed on us by circumstances or other people.

Think about it. You'll come up with some.

It's that idea that you're too old or too young, or it may be your fears and doubts, past failures, or empty pockets. Even physical barriers and disabilities are artificial limitations because they don't rob us of our freedom to make the best of what we have and of what we are.

The real limitations have to do with the way we see ourselves in the world.

What limits us is our negative outlook, the excuses we offer, pettiness, inflexibility, worry, procrastination, laziness, lack of self-discipline, bad habits, and feeling sorry for ourselves.

Those are the real limitations. When you think about those examples, you realize it's our attitudes that hold us back from becoming all that we were created to be.

Olympic skater Scott Hamilton said it perfectly: "The only disability in life is a bad attitude."

God breathed into your nostrils and gave you life. Take advantage of it.

BE THE BUTTERFLY

JANUARY 4

To move from mediocrity to excellence, you have to undergo changes as profound as the metamorphosis of a caterpillar into a butterfly.

A butterfly is not just a caterpillar with wings. It's an entirely different kind of creature. Similarly, successful people are not just failures with money. They're entirely different individuals, with different attitudes and behaviors than those who are less successful.

Becoming the butterfly you want to be means putting the old circumstances behind and focusing all your resources on creating new circumstances for yourself.

This can be risky and scary. You're leaving the comfort and security of the old cocoon and accepting the challenges and uncertainties of freedom.

It's natural to want to leave the path open for a return to the old ways if the new ones don't work out. But if you leave the path open, you're quite likely to retrace it. At the first sign of adversity, you'll give up the adventure and return to your cocoon—the life you were trying to put behind you.

A butterfly can't return to its cocoon. The moment it reaches the outside and flutters its wings, it is committed to a new type of existence. Its life as a butterfly is not just a matter of what it does; it is also a matter of what it **is**. So is your life as a successful individual.

YOUR FRIENDS, YOUR FUTURE

JANUARY 5

W ho you spend time with is who you become."
My mother told me that long ago, when I was very young. I still remember it because it has become one of the truisms of my life.

I've learned that when you associate with achievers, you are very likely to end up acting and thinking like an achiever, and will probably become one.

So, make sure the friends you associate with have positive attitudes and good habits. Cultivate friends not because of what **they** can do for **you** but for what **you** can absorb from **them**.

If you want to be great, you must first walk hand in hand and side by side with great people. Not only must you walk with them; you must also study them, emulating their successes and learning from their mistakes.

You can walk with great people through personal acquaintance and by reading their biographies. Their examples can help you recognize and analyze the failures and extract ideas and ways to do better next time.

I did this in my own life. I remember meeting William Horney, a business leader in High Point, when he was in his early nineties. We became friends, and through observation and conversation, he helped me become a better leader.

So, when you look for a crowd to hang with, look for people like William Horney. When it comes to choosing friends, it pays to aim high.

LIFE IS A COFFEE CUP

JANUARY 6

A group of alumni visited their old university professor, and conversation soon turned to complaints about stress in work and life.

The professor offered her former students coffee and returned with a large pot and an assortment of cups: porcelain, plastic, glass, and crystal—some plain-looking, some expensive, some exquisite.

She told them to help themselves. She noticed all her former students picked up the expensive, nice-looking cups, not the ones that looked plain. That, she said, was the source of their problems and pain. "Be assured that the cup itself adds no quality to the coffee," she said. "What all of you really wanted was coffee—not the cup—but you consciously went for the best cups. And then you began eyeing each other's cups."

Life is like the coffee. Our careers, money, and positions in society are like the cups. They are just tools to hold and contain life and do not define, nor change the quality of life we live.

The happiest people don't **have** the best of everything. They just **make** the best of everything.

YOUR PATH TOWARD CHANGE

JANUARY 7

Pain and pleasure. It's hard to think of them together, but you should.

For example, you may not have liked getting out of bed this morning. But you did because the pain of losing your job is greater than the pain of throwing off the covers and climbing out of bed.

Or think about your next trip to the dentist. You may not want to go, but the pain of a toothache is greater than the pain of a drill.

Or maybe a friend recommends a hike up to Green Knob in North Carolina's Pisgah National Forest; it's a tough hike, nine miles long through brush and hills. But once you make it, you find a spectacular view of a valley that will take your breath away.

Now, think about your life.

Pleasure and pain can work to motivate you toward change. When you decide that you **don't** want your future to be a repetition of your **past**, think of all the things you dislike about your present circumstances. Dwell on the pain. Then visualize the pleasures.

Here's the thing: associating pleasure with change and pain with the rut you're in will help energize you toward a commitment to change.

YE OF LITTLE FAITH

JANUARY 8

There were two friends, Bob and Tom.

Bob would tell his friends he could never cheer up, and even if he did, he knew things would get worse. And for him, they did.

But his buddy, Tom, was totally different. He could see a forecast for rain coming, and he would only think about how it would help his backyard garden grow.

It all goes back to faith. If you have faith that something good will happen, something good **will** happen. But you have to really believe—really **believe**—that good will blossom from bad.

Look at what happened with Bob and Tom. People loved Tom and avoided Bob. People even told Bob they were afraid lightning might strike them or a tree might fall on them if they were around him.

Those people thought it might just happen. Who would want to live like that? *You* wouldn't.

Just remember who calmed the storm in this verse from the book of Matthew about Jesus and the disciples at the Sea of Galilee:

"He replied, 'You of little faith, why are you so afraid?' Then he got up and rebuked the winds and the waves, and it was completely calm."

Jesus and faith. Those two go together.

AND WITH GOD...

JANUARY 9

No mountain is too high to keep you from climbing it.

No obstacle is too awesome to keep you from overcoming it.

No goal is too great to keep you from reaching it.

No problem is too difficult to keep you from solving it.

No adversary is too powerful to keep you from conquering it.

No burden is too heavy to keep you from bearing it.

No aspiration is too noble to keep you from attaining it.

—William A. Ward

THREE BIG QUESTIONS

JANUARY 10

I t sounds so simple. That is, until you try to find an answer. In choosing a purpose in life, sit down at a laptop or grab a legal pad and answer three big questions:

Who am I? This will help you focus. Write a short essay of a few hundred words. Don't mention your name, age, educational background, or biographical information. It's not a résumé. Ask yourself the only question that really matters: Who are you as a person?

What am I doing here? This has nothing to do with location. It has everything to do with what you can contribute to make this world a better place. Write an epitaph for yourself and reduce it to a few words. How do you want people to remember you?

Where am I going? Just one sentence, that's all. What direction will you pursue in life? Then rate yourself on a scale of one to ten about how you measure up.

These are big questions. But remember a career offers not only money but also meaning. At the same time, personal and family relationships bring love to your life, community and religious goals satisfy your spiritual and altruistic needs, and cultural and recreational goals make it fun to live.

So sit down. Think. Then write it down. It's worth it.

RUN, CHARLIE, RUN

JANUARY 11

A football coach once trained a talented player named Charlie as a running back. He taught him all the skills and moves. In the key game against a huge, aggressive defense, the coach told the quarterback, "Give the ball to Charlie."

On the first play, the quarterback faked a handoff to Charlie but kept the ball—and was clobbered by the defensive line.

"Give the ball to Charlie," yelled the coach.

Again and again, the quarterback faked the handoff, kept the ball, and was creamed. On fourth down and twenty, the coach finally called his quarterback to the sidelines.

"I thought I told you to give the ball to Charlie," he said.

"I know, Coach," replied the quarterback, "but Charlie says he doesn't **want** the ball."

Never hand the ball to someone who doesn't want it. Consider the thoughts and feelings of the people you deal with. If you detect a reluctance to carry the ball, hand it to someone else who **wants** to carry it. And find some other way for Charlie to contribute to the cause.

BE THE STEAM BOILER

JANUARY 12

G enius is 1 percent inspiration and 99 percent perspiration."

Thomas Edison said that. He invented the lightbulb, the phonograph, and the motion picture camera, all tools endemic to who we are today.

But those inventions didn't come about from just a flash of inspiration. It takes months or years of perspiration, but it shows that people with seemingly ordinary gifts can make extraordinary contributions to society.

The secret? You must determine where your strengths lie and then focus them on your objectives.

Focus is the key word. It is simply a way of mobilizing and concentrating power. Take the water in a steam boiler. It has no more potential than the water in your shower. But the water in the steam boiler, when energized and focused, can propel locomotives. The unfocused, nonenergized water in the bathtub just goes down the drain.

Think about this quote from Thomas Wolfe, the legendary writer from North Carolina:

"If a man has a talent and cannot use it, he has failed. If he has a talent and only uses half of it, he has partly failed. If he has a talent and learns to use the whole of it, he has gloriously succeeded, and won a satisfaction and triumph few men will know."

So identify your talent. You'll "gloriously succeed."

LET THE MOTH BE

JANUARY 13

Once, a little girl watched a moth trying to struggle free from its cocoon. Seeking to help the beautiful creature, she reached into her pocket and pulled out her knife. Ever so carefully, she cut away the cocoon and freed the moth.

For a long time, she watched the moth as it flapped its wings and tried unsuccessfully to fly. Finally, the wings sagged for the last time, and the moth died.

The little girl was crushed. Her older sister tried to help. She said, "The struggle gives strength to the moth's wings. When you cut away the cocoon, you took away the very exercise that would have enabled it to fly."

Of course, none of us like to struggle with difficulties and misfortunes, but a wise person accepts them as opportunities to grow. Wise and self-confident people welcome the struggle—the resistance—because they know it is the best way to develop character.

FLY LIKE A BUMBLEBEE

JANUARY 14

There are some who say that the bumblebee greatly overestimates her ability to fly. Her body is much too large for the flimsy set of wings nature gave her. But the bumblebee thinks she can fly, she flaps her wings as if she **expects** to fly, and guess what…

She **flies**, and she flies very well.

One of the greatest mistakes you can make is to underestimate yourself. It's far worse to underestimate than it is to overestimate.

The reason is quite simple: you act in harmony with the way you see yourself.

So take a tip from the bumblebee. Visualize yourself as someone who can fly. Then put those wings in motion and soar!

ANGELS IN FLIGHT
JANUARY 15

A bishop was accustomed to paying an annual visit to a small religious college. On one such visit, the bishop engaged in an after-dinner conversation with the college president.

The religious leader offered the opinion that the millennium could not be long in coming since everything about nature had been discovered and all possible inventions had been made.

The college president disagreed, stating that he felt the next fifty years would bring amazing discoveries and inventions. In his opinion, within a relatively short time, human beings would be flying through the skies like birds.

"Nonsense!" protested the bishop. "Flight is reserved for the angels!"

The bishop's name was Wright. He had two sons, Orville and Wilbur.

There are no such things as unrealistic dreams, only unrealistic time lines.

THE BUSINESS MIND-SET YOU NEED

JANUARY 16

In your career, you can see yourself in one of two ways—a worker or an entrepreneur. You don't have to be an hourly employee to have a worker mentality. And you don't have to be an independent businessperson to have an entrepreneurial mentality.

It's the basic attitude—not the occupational category—that counts. Those who follow the worker mentality do not discern a clear connection between their own success and the success of the company. If the company's performance is marginal, they are not overly concerned so long as they continue to draw paychecks and receive their annual increases. They may attend to their own areas competently, but they do not worry about what happens outside their areas of responsibility.

Those who follow the entrepreneurial mentality see themselves as partners in prosperity with the company. They view the company's ups and downs as **their** ups and downs and are constantly looking for things that they personally can do to contribute to the company's profitability. They see the company as an institution with no boundaries and look for ways they can make a difference in all aspects of its operations.

A company with a workforce full of entrepreneurs is almost sure to **succeed**, and the entrepreneurs will share in its success.

Think like **that**, and you can share in the success wherever you are.

CROSS YOUR RIVER

JANUARY 17

To build your **dream**, you first must cross your own personal Rubicon. But first, a quick lesson in linguistics and history.

To cross your Rubicon means to take a step from which there is no turning back. The expression springs from the actions of Julius Caesar when he was in command of a provincial Roman army in 49 BC.

Caesar knew that Roman law forbade him to lead his army outside its assigned province. But he wanted more than a provincial command. He wanted to rule the empire. The boundary of Caesar's province was the Rubicon River in northern Italy. He knew that if he crossed the Rubicon he would have no choice but to continue on to Rome and conquer or be conquered.

Caesar crossed the Rubicon and reportedly cried out, "Let us go where the omens of the Gods and the crimes of our enemies summon us! The die is now cast!"

The rest is history.

To seal your commitment and march successfully into the future, you have to cross your own Rubicon. The future is a place you've never been before, and many people are more than a little nervous about entering it.

They prefer the **safe**, familiar circumstances of the past. But if you are trying constantly to relive the familiar **past**, you'll never enjoy the rewarding future.

The way to keep from reliving the past is to take that irrevocable step. Cut yourself off from past circumstances so that your only choice is to move ahead.

When you move with that kind of commitment, providence **moves** too. You will find all kinds of ways to make the dream you created come true.

KING LOOKED THE PART OF A LEADER

JANUARY 18

When people saw Martin Luther King Jr., they didn't see a wisecracking, street-talking radical. They saw a dignified man, dressed conservatively and tastefully, who spoke of freedom and justice.

When such a man is beaten and jailed, the national conscience recoils. Take the tumultuous year of 1965. Dr. King fought for voting rights in the face of bigotry, and on the steps of the state capitol in Montgomery, Alabama, he took his message to the people—and to the nation. He said, "We must come to see that the end we seek is a society at peace with itself, a society that can live with its conscience. And that will be a day not of the white man, not of the black man. That will be the day of man as man."

A few months later, in the presence of Dr. King and other civil rights leader, President Lyndon Johnson signed the Voting Rights Act of 1965.

King's words worked. But he spoke not only with words but also with his attitude and his appearance. He knew that he was constantly onstage, and he saw to it that the image he projected reinforced the verbal message he was sending.

It was a message that changed the course of America.

THE LAW OF LIFE

JANUARY 19

How do you think of your life—as a machine or as an organism?

The way you think about it has a great deal to do with the way you manage it.

A machine can be dealt with one part at a time. An organism demands an integrated approach because its parts are interdependent and complementary.

An organism is a living thing. It has the power to evolve, to transform itself, to change from within.

A machine is inanimate. It has no control over itself. It can only respond to outside controls.

Organisms can adapt to their environments. Machines function only in fixed patterns. Organisms can learn. Machines can't.

If you expect to survive in an era of rapid change, you must transform your life into a living, thinking, evolving organism. You must equip yourself to adapt to a changing environment and to take the initiative to change the environment itself.

Consider what John F. Kennedy once said: "Change is the law of life. And those who look only to the past or the present are certain to miss the future."

KNOW ONE ANOTHER

JANUARY 20

T he next time you have a conversation with a friend, remember this: dialogue means more than swapping opinions.

If your friend says the United States is a democracy, and you say, "No, it's not!" and then you both drop the subject, nothing is accomplished. You and your friend have swapped opinions, but neither of you has gained insight into how the other thinks.

But suppose you explain that the United States isn't a democracy where all issues are settled by public vote, but rather a republic where elected representatives make laws.

But then your friend counters by saying a democracy is a government where people have a right to choose their representatives by popular vote.

Now we're getting somewhere; it's a civics lesson. In this conversation, you realize the similarities between your views are greater than your differences. Then you can move on.

But it's more than that. As the scientist Albert Einstein said, "Any fool can know. The point is to understand."

And that's especially important whether it's between you and your friend or between you and a roomful of people.

Understanding is the key to obtaining knowledge.

WHEN FAILURE LEADS TO SUCCESS

JANUARY 21

T hink about the basic skills you've acquired in life.

You learned to walk by pulling yourself up and then turning loose and taking a step. You fell the first time. But you got up and tried again. Each time, you did it a little better until you could walk by yourself.

You learned by doing with every activity, whether tying your shoes or driving a car. With each endeavor, you started as a novice and learned from your mistakes.

The same can be said for your goals. You will make mistakes, but that's okay. Learn from them. That's what successful people do. They know the difference between a productive failure and a nonproductive success.

In a productive failure, you don't achieve your objective. But you come away from the experience with new knowledge and understanding that will increase your chances of success on the next try.

A nonproductive success occurs when you achieve your objective, but you're not sure what you did right.

The more actions you take, the more productive failures you'll experience…and the more you'll learn.

Thomas Edison experienced 1,100 productive failures before he found the right filament for his incandescent lamp.

Just think about what you could achieve with your own bright ideas.

THE BULLDOZER'S LESSON

JANUARY 22

When he saw the bulldozer demolishing an old house on the other side of town, the architect stopped his white pickup and remembered.

Many years ago on his first job, he operated a bulldozer. But today, he spends his days away from machines that once spurred his imagination to dream big.

The architect got out of his pickup, and when the bulldozer's operator saw him, he stopped.

"Can I help you?" he asked.

"How much horsepower does that thing have?" the architect yelled.

"Sixty," the operator said, smiling. "I'll bet you're thinking your big pickup has more than four times the horses."

"You're right," the man responded.

"But your pickup won't demolish buildings," the operator said. "The difference is in the transmission. It's not the power that counts; it's how you use it. This baby's geared for power."

All of us have more power in our minds, personalities, and talents than we can ever use. We just have to learn to apply that power effectively.

There is no secret to it. You have to focus on activities that contribute to the greatest value in your life and do more of those, while eliminating the activities that contribute little or no value to your life and are a meaningless investment of your energy.

As Mahatma Gandhi said, "There is more to life than simply increasing its speed."

DON'T SETTLE

JANUARY 23

To live excellently is to be extraordinary.

People who value excellence won't tolerate lax standards. Ordinary people regard a 99 percent quality standard as quite good, and maybe a little too demanding.

But how would you feel if you made a $1,000 deposit and your bank credited you with only $990?

That's 99 percent accuracy.

Or how would you feel if the interest on your home mortgage came to $5,000 a year and you were charged $5,050?

That's 99 percent accuracy as well.

If everyone adhered to the 99 percent standard, we would be without telephone service for fifteen minutes each day. We'd find about three misspelled words on each page we read. Doctors and nurses would drop thirty-five thousand newborn babies a year, two hundred thousand people would get the wrong drug prescriptions, and two million people would die of food poisoning.

Don't settle for 99 percent or even 99.9 percent. Go for the whole nine yards. You don't have to be a superhero to perform the extraordinary.

All you need is a commitment to doing more than ordinary people do.

THE THREE Fs YOU NEED
JANUARY 24

Common sense tells us that success often revolves around the **three Fs of achievement**: If you have your **fans**, your **fame**, and your **fortune**, you've really done something. What a sad way to measure life's accomplishments.

Uncommon sense tells us that significance revolves about **the three Fs of appreciation**: **faith, family,** and **friends**. Those who have a sufficient supply of faith, family, and friends live life more fully and at a higher level than most people ever reach.

How do you identify the role that offers the best opportunity to use your talents significantly?

Here are some questions that will help begin the process:

- What is the guiding or controlling idea in my life?
- What is my strategy for implementing that idea?
- What are my three greatest strengths, and what am I doing to capitalize on them?
- What are my three greatest weaknesses, and what am I doing to compensate for them?

Answer these questions today. You'll have a pretty clear picture of who you are and what your most valuable assets are. Then you can find a role that will utilize your greatest strengths without being hampered by your greatest weaknesses.

IT WON'T HURT—IF YOU HOLD IT RIGHT

JANUARY 25

A gardener known for his flowers loves giving his roses away because he believes it's a way to show friendship and caring through beauty. Once, when he tried to hand a gorgeous rose to a close friend, the friend seemed more aware of the thorns on the stem than he did the rose.

But the gardener stopped his friend and showed him how to grasp the rose right below the flower so his friend wouldn't get hurt.

"If you know how to hold it, it won't hurt you," he told him.

A moment of life is like that, isn't it?

If you know how to find the good in it, even a sad moment can't hurt you.

Instead, it will bring you joy, increase your faith, and help you to focus on the beauty of the world.

OUTSIDE YOUR FRONT DOOR

JANUARY 26

National and world leaders are shaped and formed in their local communities. Even the path to the White House can start in a neighborhood with the humblest beginnings. For example, Harry Truman was a postmaster before he was president. Lyndon Johnson was a schoolteacher. William McKinley was a postal clerk and a country schoolteacher. Bill Clinton was a sax-playing teenager whose stepfather was an abusive alcoholic. Barack Obama is the son of divorced parents.

All of them rose to the presidency by becoming actively involved in their communities.

Volunteer. Be involved. As Calvin Coolidge said, "Service is the rent we pay for the space we occupy on earth."

LISTEN...AND LEARN

JANUARY 27

It's easy to think of communication as a way of sending messages. But sending is only half the process. Receiving is the other half.

So, at some point, we have to stop sending and prepare to receive.

It's like Lyndon Johnson said, "You aren't learning anything when you're talking."

We receive information with more than our ears. Our eyes play key roles as well. They convey the body language that often tells us what feelings accompany the words we're hearing. If we're going to communicate effectively, we must learn to stop, look, and listen.

"It takes two to speak the truth," said Henry David Thoreau, "one to speak, and another to hear."

You can't hear unless you stop—and listen.

KEEP YOUR TORCH LIT

JANUARY 28

Losers see themselves as doing a job. Winners see themselves as a part of all humankind and their work as their contribution to a better world.

George Bernard Shaw, the great English playwright, put it this way: "I am convinced that my life belongs to the whole community; and as long as I live, it is my privilege to do for it whatever I can, for the harder I work, the more I live. I rejoice in life for its own sake. Life is no brief candle for me. It is a sort of splendid torch which I got hold of for a moment, and I want to make it burn as brightly as possible before turning it over to future generations."

Can you imagine life ever being boring, or work dull, for a person with such a spirit?

We all can be like that. You have a light worthy of sharing with the world.

Make sure we all see it.

THE DOCTRINE OF "AND THEN SOME"

JANUARY 29

Have you been in a race and come to a point where you couldn't take another step? Has your schedule ever been so full that you knew you couldn't find time to do anything else?

But in each case, you didn't let that stop you. You finished the race, and you made time in your schedule to meet with someone because you felt it was the right thing to do.

You do all you can…and then some.

When you're sizing up your capacities, allow for the "and then some." It can provide you with positive stress that enables you to meet the challenge.

And then some.

HUMOR: A WELCOME SUMMER RAIN

JANUARY 30

All it takes is ten minutes.

A recent study from Vanderbilt University shows that ten to fifteen minutes of laughter a day can burn up to fifty calories. Another study from the University of Maryland discovered a sense of humor can protect you against heart disease.

Experts on stress point out that a good sense of humor is a strong defense against being overcome by cortisol, the stress hormone.

The person who can laugh often, and who finds humor in even the most stressful events, can keep going when others are falling.

So find a way to laugh and include it in your daily routine. People enjoy being around those who have a good sense of humor.

As the poet Langston Hughes believed: "Like a welcome summer rain, humor may suddenly cleanse and cool the earth, the air, and you."

WHAT SOLITUDE LOVES

JANUARY 31

To put yourself in a creative mood, find a time and place that allows you to be alone and undisturbed.

Some find it in the solitude of a mountain cabin, while others find it during long walks on the beach, casting for bass in a secluded lake, or in a favorite nook right in their own homes.

Wherever you find it, use solitude as your gateway to the world of creative imagination. Don't concentrate.

Just open your mind and let your thoughts and ideas enter on the wings of inspiration.

FEBRUARY

WAKE UP!

FEBRUARY 1

Why would anyone want to wake up to an **alarm** clock?

Think of it not as an alarm clock. Instead, think of it as an **opportunity** clock that wakes you up and you think, "Good morning, Lord! What a great day!"

With that kind of attitude, you have already made a choice about what kind of day it will be.

Your beliefs lead to your behaviors, and behaviors dictate your results. If you don't like the results, don't fuss about your behaviors. Examine and realign your beliefs.

Think "I can," "I will," and "I believe differently."

"Successful and unsuccessful people do not vary greatly in their abilities," says John Maxwell, a minister and bestselling writer. "They vary in their desires to reach their potential."

IT IS IMPORTANT TO DREAM

FEBRUARY 2

For every truly great innovation, at least one hundred could probably have been made but never were. Why?

Two reasons: many potential innovators failed to dream, and many dreamers failed to make their dreams become reality.

But not Steve Wozniak.

He, along with Steve Jobs and Ronald Wayne, created Apple Computer, Inc. They dreamed about it and made it happen because Wozniak believed a computer could empower people and make life easier.

He talked about creating the first Apple computers during his commencement speech at High Point University, where he also serves on its National Board of Advisors.

"Very often we look at something we have and say, 'I could make it better,'" he told the graduates. "That's innovation. But you know what? Sometimes we say, 'I could do something totally different that makes things a lot easier for people,' and that's true invention. It is important to dream."

What do you dream about?

ALWAYS BE YOURSELF

FEBRUARY 3

A sign once spotted in a rural North Carolina store provided sound advice: "Be who you is, because when you is who you ain't, you ain't who you is."

A short adjective for people who try to be who they aren't is "phony." Nobody likes a phony.

Be yourself, but be your **best** self. When you dislike yourself, it's hard to like others— and it's even harder for others to like you.

TWO KEY WORDS

FEBRUARY 4

C hange can be confronted with an air of resignation or of challenge. If you accept it with resignation, you're at the mercy of change. If you accept it as a challenge, change is your creative instrument.

Creativity is often assumed to be an inborn trait, but it can be learned. Your creative energies often can be ignited by two words.

What's next?

That phrase puts the ball in future's court and calls for change. It keeps you from being married to an unproductive idea. If you say, "This isn't working; what's next?" your mind immediately begins searching for another solution.

Knowledge is to creativity what a bed of coals is to a fire. It provides a reservoir of resources to keep the creative fires burning.

To develop creativity, acquire a thirst for knowledge. Read, travel, and explore. Browse through libraries, bookstores, and magazine racks. Savor new places and new experiences.

Share your knowledge with other people and ask them to share theirs with you. Be open to innovative thinking and innovative procedures, regardless of where they originate.

NO WAY

FEBRUARY 5

The stories of most of the truly great achievements of history almost always start with these words: "They said it couldn't be done!"

Consider Roger Bannister. No one thought a person could run a mile in under four minutes. But Bannister did it in 1954. Since then, many runners have run the mile in less than four minutes.

Similarly, no one thought that sending a man to the moon would happen except in science fiction. But on July 20, 1969, Neil Armstrong took that "one small step for a man, one giant leap for mankind."

Or consider Malala Yousafzai. No one even thought a teenager could have a chance at winning the Nobel Peace Prize. But on December 10, 2014, she became the youngest recipient of the Nobel Peace Prize since it was first awarded in 1901.

Yousafzai was honored for her advocacy of educating young women in Pakistan. She started her work after Taliban fighters shut down her school and shot her in the head in 2012.

When she won the Nobel Peace Prize, she was only seventeen.

"This award is not just for me," she said. "It is for those forgotten children who want education. It is for the frightened children who want peace. It is for those voiceless children who want change."

The key to success? It is a firm faith that it **could** be done and the confident expectation that it **would** be done.

FRUITFUL FAILURE

FEBRUARY 6

L earn to think about your mistakes and failures in the proper perspective. The key lies in tying your sense of personal security to something deeper than immediate success. You can build and maintain your self-confidence by balancing your mistakes against your long-term goals, underlying purpose in life, and inherent worth as a human being, rather than against their immediate consequences.

No mistake you could ever make would strip you of your value as a human being. Most mistakes detour you only slightly on your road to fulfilling your purpose in life.

Remember this: Mistakes are seldom fatal. It's your attitude toward mistakes that can cost you.

Those who can come out of each mistake or failure better equipped to face the future are able not only to salvage self-confidence, but also to build it even stronger.

Think of the Japanese proverb. It says much in seven simple words: "Fall down seven times. Stand up eight."

MAKE YOUR UNCONSCIOUS MIND YOUR FRIEND

FEBRUARY 7

It's your unconscious mind that counts.

The unconscious mind believes what the conscious mind tells it. When a conscious thought flits through your mind, your unconscious mind "hears" it, believes it, and records it. Your conscious mind may forget about it immediately, but it's on permanent file in your unconscious.

Your unconscious mind is the storehouse for your habits—all the things you do without consciously thinking about them.

Therefore, your unconscious mind has a profound effect on the way you act.

For example, if you think, "I'll never learn how to use Excel," your unconscious mind believes you and acts as a roadblock from learning that software.

If you think, "I'll never get out of this dead-end job," your unconscious mind will perceive that you are stuck.

Pessimists always feed their unconscious minds with negative thoughts, and their pessimism becomes a self-fulfilling prophecy.

Make a conscious decision to allow yourself only to think positive thoughts about yourself every day. Think of your perceptions like a coin. Each thought has a "head" and a "tail." Successful people learn to flip their coins to the other side and see optimism wherever they go.

YOU NEED A PLAN

FEBRUARY 8

To create your future, you must have a vision and express it through a mission statement. Write it down and post it in a place where you can see it every day. Once you do, your dream glitters on the horizon of the future.

Standing in the reality of the here and now, you can't dream your way to the future. You need a plan to know where you want to go and how you're going to get there.

The important word is "how." To achieve your vision, you must approach it with a positive attitude—and a sense of certainty that your dream is achievable.

A plan with these characteristics is essential:

- ✺ It specifies actions.
- ✺ It sets a timetable.
- ✺ It is flexible and can be amended it when necessary.

Start planning today and see how it affects you. And remember this from Confucius, the Chinese philosopher: "A man who does not plan long ahead will find trouble right at his door."

THE DANCE OF YOUR LEFT AND RIGHT

FEBRUARY 9

Your vision springs from the creative right side of your brain. To create a workable action plan, you need to bring the left side of the brain into the picture to pass ultimate judgment on your ideas and set priorities.

Begin the planning process by revisiting your vision and reviewing the mission statement you wrote.

Assess your present circumstances and measure the gap between where you are and where you want to be. Then follow these steps:

- Set goals.
- Set priorities.
- Develop strategies.

As you develop your plan, keep this point in mind: your present circumstances do not control your options.

They establish a starting point, but they don't determine your destination. Where you are very quickly becomes where you've been. So keep your eyes focused on the future instead of on the past. Focus on where you want to go rather than where you've been. Have a good trip.

THE MOST VALUABLE LESSON

FEBRUARY 10

A young man, armed with his new MBA, dropped in on his old college professor to ask him a question that had stuck with him since graduate school.

"I know a master's degree alone doesn't guarantee success," he said. "What do you think is the most important quality for someone who wants to become a business leader?"

His old professor answered without hesitation—the ability to communicate. The old professor shut his laptop, got up from his chair, sat on the edge of his desk, and began to teach a class of one.

"Today," he said, "a leader is not a transmitter of commands but a creator of motivational environments, and workers are not robots, but thinking individuals pouring their ingenuity into the organization's purpose."

The three keys, the professor said, are desire, understanding the process, and mastering the basic skills. "The communications that endure," he said, "don't come from an exhaustive vocabulary, but from plain, simple language.

"The leader who can't communicate can't create the conditions that motivate, and the genius who can't communicate is intellectually impotent," said the professor, raising his voice for emphasis. "The organization that can't communicate can't change, and the organization that can't change is dead."

THE REAL WORLD

FEBRUARY 11

B ill Gates loved making software. He helped create Microsoft, and he became one of the richest people in the world.

But he and his wife, Melinda, wanted to do more. In 2000, they created the Bill & Melinda Gates Foundation to help solve some of the world's biggest problems.

On the foundation's blog, they write, "We believe that every person deserves the chance to live a healthy, productive life."

People will always try to pull you down to their level. But you must shun that. The real world is the one you create for yourself and others.

Bill and Melinda Gates did that. They want to create a world the way things ought to be.

Their blog title says it all: *Impatient Optimists.*

INFORMATION ALONE IS LIFELESS

FEBRUARY 12

T he twenty-first century requires an ability to communicate freely, precisely, and clearly. This kind of communication cannot be accomplished solely by microchips, fiber optics, and satellite relays. These artifacts of our technology help to fill the world with information, but information is lifeless without someone to breathe meaning into it.

That someone can be you. How will you do it?

One person at a time. Every day.

KEEP YOUR COMPASS CLOSE

FEBRUARY 13

Your principles can be like a compass, quickly pointing in the right direction when crisis arrives.

They can be like an anchor, providing a source of steadiness amid tumultuous circumstances.

Or they can be like the nozzle of a hose, directing the stream of your thoughts and efforts in a purposeful way while concentrating their power on the things that matter.

Here's how George Packer, author of *The Unwinding: An Inner History of the New America*, the 2013 winner of the National Book Award, described principles: "Ideology knows the answer before the question has been asked. Principles are something different: a set of values that have to be adapted to circumstances but not compromised away."

Your compass is calibrated by your principles. That is the foundation of what you have become. In any crisis, you need that kind of solid support.

We all do.

USE THE MOST POWERFUL FORCE IN THE UNIVERSE

FEBRUARY 14

O f all the human abilities, love is the noblest.

It is by far the most powerful force in the universe. Love moves the spirit to create, the mind to think, and the body to perform.

Hate may be a strong force, as are self-centered egotism, apathy, and fear. However, nothing can lift you to the heights enjoyed by those who respond to the love within and the love from others.

Only love can make all your success worthwhile. Whatever else you cultivate, cultivate love.

Only when you love and are loved can you reach your full potential as a human being.

As English poet Robert Browning once said, "Without love, our earth is a tomb."

A CARD GAME TO PLAY

FEBRUARY 15

The principle that success begets success is a valid one.

Each challenge you meet and overcome uncovers new challenges. Successfully tackling obstacles strengthens you to meet the next roadblock in your path.

Successful people have learned to establish a pattern of successful action. Succeeding in small things builds confidence, creating an expectation of success that becomes a self-fulfilling prophecy.

As in baseball, you can build on yesterday's success or put the game's failures behind you. Then, you can start all over again.

"Baseball is like a poker game," said baseball great Jackie Robinson. "Nobody wants to quit when he's losing; nobody wants you to quit when you're ahead."

To find your own cards of **success**:

- Find a core motivation, one built around a set of positive principles that are important to you.
- Identify the area where you effectively influence others and let those principles motivate you and guide your actions.
- Identify the things you can change and go about changing them.
- Identify the things you can't change and develop positive strategies for dealing with them.
- Ignore the trivial.

As H. Jackson Brown wrote in *Life's Little Instruction Book*, "Don't stop the parade to pick up a dime."

WRITING YOUR OWN SET OF RULES

FEBRUARY 16

History books and entertainment magazines are full of examples of people whose careers soared while their lives crashed—even as they were doing the things they excelled at and enjoyed.

This can happen if your behavior is not in line with rules of conduct based on a set of principles grounded in positive personal values.

But don't look for a set of rules for what you can and can't do in life. Write your own rules based on the principles you choose and the values you cherish.

First, some things to remember: A value is something you hold dear. A principle is a broad, fundamental truth. A rule of conduct is a guide to behavior designed to implement a principle.

For example, consider this: Human life has value. "It is wrong to take a human life deliberately and maliciously" is a principle. "Thou shall not commit murder" is a rule of conduct.

The principle supports the value; the rule implements the principle. Different people value different things. You may view some values as negative and some as positive. Some people value generosity, kindness, and decency. Others value greed, violence, and obscenity.

What you value determines the principles by which you measure your behavior.

FIVE THINGS TO REMEMBER

FEBRUARY 17

Here are five common causes of failure in personal relationships, whether in business or at home. They are:

- ✦ **Preoccupation with self.** The word "success" does not contain an "I." The first vowel is "u," and until we learn to think **you** instead of **I**, our batting average in business and in human relations will be close to zero.
- ✦ **Hasty assumptions.** People who jump to conclusions rarely land in the middle of success.
- ✦ **Negative attitudes.** Some people bring on their bad luck through negative attitudes. They know things are going to go wrong, and this faith becomes a self-fulfilling prophecy.
- ✦ **A disregard for courtesy.** It never works.
- ✦ **A desire to be liked.** When you try to buy friendship at any price, you cheapen the product. You end up not respecting yourself, and others don't respect you either. You win respect by setting high standards and living up to them.

The best rule for human interaction is still the one pronounced nearly two thousand years ago from a hillside in Galilee: "As ye would that men should do to you, do ye also to them likewise."

JUST ASK

FEBRUARY 18

Matthew Lewis grew up in a small coal-mining town in Pennsylvania. He drove a cab, pounded railroad spikes, and served as a medic in the navy and marines before returning home to work in a foundry, sandblasting steel.

But he always wanted to be a photographer. His dad was a photographer, as was his grandfather, and when he didn't get a raise at the foundry, he became a photographer too.

Lewis started hanging out at his grandfather's studio, studied photography at a school in New York, and came back to become the public relations photographer for a local college.

He eventually wound up at the *Washington Post*, one of the world's most influential newspapers, where he won a Pulitzer Prize for feature photography in 1975.

And what started it all? The advice he received from famous photographer Gordon Parks about how to become a news photographer.

What a difference mentors can make. Always learn from the experts because they have their knowledge from their own experience. Otherwise, while you may learn more, you won't have the benefit of years of experience from those who have traveled the path before you.

OVERCOMING FAILURE

FEBRUARY 19

Successful people know that failure is a temporary thing. In his poem "If," Rudyard Kipling listed among the ingredients of manhood the ability to

> *Watch the things you gave your life to, broken,*
> *And stoop and build 'em up with worn-out tools*

Failure has been the prelude to many a success story. Truly successful people learn to turn each failure into a positive experience. They find out why they failed and then use this knowledge to move toward success.

So what is success?

It's finding and doing what you enjoy most to the best of your ability every moment of your life.

Are you doing that?

TO BE HUMAN...

FEBRUARY 20

C ommunication is a human activity, not a mechanical function. Communication is focused on establishing meaning and understanding by sharing feelings, desires, needs, and ideas. Machines can only process information. But they can't provide meaning and understanding. The most extraordinary people know the difference. They dedicate their lives to building bridges of understanding with others. They speak less, listen more, and show an ample supply of empathy.

TRACTORS THAT WOULDN'T PULL

FEBRUARY 21

During the Maoist period in China, before the mainland opened itself to Western ideas, the Chinese built their own tractors.

Engineers who were taught to build engines, transmissions, and chassis had designed them. But these were engineers, not farmers. In ancient Chinese cultures, educated people such as engineers would not condescend to do a farmer's work.

These engineers had never worked on farms and had never driven farm tractors. So they had only vague concepts about the specific tasks these tractors would have to perform.

When the tractors arrived at the farms, the farmers immediately saw a defect the engineers hadn't detected. The tractors had no drawbars—the bars at the rear to which they could attach the equipment they pulled. Without drawbars, the tractors were useless for pulling plows and other equipment.

In time, the Chinese learned to bring lofty designs down to the level of the plow and the furrow. They found that it is pointless to assemble a mass of technical expertise unless they also acquire the knowledge of how this expertise can be used to meet human needs.

Being pragmatic is an asset.

CHOOSE EXCELLENCE

FEBRUARY 22

T he difference between the behavior of high achievers and mediocre performers, especially in the workplace, is interesting.

Both look to others for assistance. But the star performers form networks **before** they need assistance, and when the time comes to call for outside help, they know where to look.

On the other hand, mediocre performers wait until they need help before looking around for assistance—and it is not always there.

Dancer Martha Graham saw mediocrity as a sin. You may see it as a waste of your talent and a diminishment of your potential to achieve what is within your grasp.

Warren Bennis, a leadership expert who has advised presidents and business executives, believed that as well.

"Excellence is a better teacher than mediocrity," Bennis says. "The lessons of the ordinary are everywhere. Truly profound and original insights are to be found only in studying the exemplary."

Choose to be extraordinary.

THINK LIKE JESSE

FEBRUARY 23

T he most important person for you to understand is yourself. It's not complicated. Meet Jesse Lear, a cofounder of V.I.P. Waste Services, an Ohio company that offers door-to-door pickup of recycling and garage at apartment complexes.

Lear is under thirty. Here's what he does every night before he goes to bed: "I think about this question: If I live every day the same way I did today, what kind of future would that create? It forces me to constantly evaluate whether or not my actions are lining up with my priorities. The future is shaped one day at a time, and it's never as far away as we think."

Communicate with your inner self daily. Identify your weaknesses and shore them up. Analyze the way you think, respond, and act. Learn what your strengths are and exert them positively.

If you do these things, personal success will follow as day follows night.

YOU GOT A MINUTE?

FEBRUARY 24

Whatever it may be—a new major, a new job, a new responsibility—stop at intervals to talk to others about what you're doing.

Don't be afraid. Be honest and listen. If you encounter obstacles, share them with friends, family, and associates, and get their advice on your life's action plan.

Someone you know may have the perfect answer to your problem and make a dynamite suggestion that will help you achieve your goals more effectively.

At the very least, you may pick up the germ of an idea. That could be the very seed of your success.

THE FUTURE IS YOU

FEBRUARY 25

Many people become frightened when they perceive the end of the stable career path that has led steadily upward from diploma to gold watch.

Yet the future for today's young people holds exhilarating opportunities that were not there for previous generations.

During student orientation at High Point University, I tell parents that their children could have as many as forty-five different jobs in their lifetime. They will have to be nimble and be able to adapt because how you change is how you succeed.

People today have the opportunity to reinvent themselves over and over in exciting, new roles.

Be flexible. Take calculated risks. Develop leadership qualities. That is the key to possessing an entrepreneurial spirit.

FAILURE: A PRELUDE TO SUCCESS
FEBRUARY 26

Remember that:

- Henry Ford failed and went broke five times before he finally succeeded.
- Babe Ruth, whose home-run records stood for more than three decades, also held the record for striking out.
- Winston Churchill did not become prime minister of the United Kingdom until he was sixty-six and then only after a lifetime of defeats and setbacks.
- Eighteen publishers turned down *Jonathan Livingston Seagull*, Richard Bach's ten thousand–word story about a seagull, before Macmillan finally published it in 1970. By 1975, it had sold more than seven million copies in the United States alone.
- Richard Hooker worked for seven years on his humorous war novel, *M*A*S*H*, only to have it rejected by twenty-one publishers before Morrow decided to publish it. It became a bestseller, a blockbuster movie, and a highly successful television series.

So hang in there no matter what.

THINK POSITIVE

FEBRUARY 27

P eople rarely succeed in spite of their expectations.

Whether you expect to succeed or expect to fail, your expectations become self-fulfilling prophecies.

When you expect failure, you unconsciously communicate your expectations to your subconscious mind. It accepts the notion that you're a failure and proceeds to cause you to act like a failure. You actually program your mind to do the things that will lead you to fail.

But when you expect to succeed, well, that's different.

You unconsciously tell your subconscious that you're a successful person. Your subconscious now directs you along a course that will lead to success.

It may lead to so many things—an extra effort that could be the difference between success and failure or the move to seek out the people who can contribute to your success.

Whatever happens, your subconscious can be the catalyst that provides the spark of inspiration or intuition that produces the germ of success.

What is your subconscious working on?

FIND YOUR LIGHT

FEBRUARY 28

If you listen for words, you'll miss the message.

The spoken word is just a morsel of sound; the thoughts and feelings behind the words are what you should listen for. To capture thoughts and feelings, you must genuinely care about what the other person is saying.

"Beauty is not in the face," Lebanese poet Khalil Gibran once said. "Beauty is a light in the heart."

So listen with your mind and heart as well as with your ears.

If you do, you'll find the light.

MARCH

YODA KNOWS

MARCH 1

The value in any decision is in its implementation.

At this point, most goals break down. Ask most people to tell you on the first of March how many of their New Year's resolutions they have kept, and they will confess that they can't even remember what they were.

You can't spend money you are "going to make someday." You can't enjoy books you only "intend to read."

And you can't live on memories of ideas you once had.

Remember Yoda, the pint-sized Jedi master from *Star Wars*. He told Luke Skywalker, "Do. Or do not. There is no try."

They didn't call him a Jedi master for nothing.

GIVE ME THAT SLINGSHOT

MARCH 2

Will you move effectively toward your goals, or simply give up when different challenges appear? It often depends on the way you view what lies ahead. Israel's David had the right attitude.

"Goliath is just too big for me to fight with this little slingshot," he could have said.

Instead, he decided that the giant was too big for him to miss. That's courage. Faithful courage. It's what you need when things get tough.

Take the sign spotted outside a small town in North Carolina. In big letters, the sign read: "We hear there's a recession coming. We've decided not to participate."

David with a slingshot. A tiny town with moxie. Both great examples of faithful courage in action.

THE NEED TO LOSE YOURSELF

MARCH 3

One of our students at High Point University made a recent discovery about High Point, her hometown. As a student at HPU, she ended up volunteering at a community center in an area of the city she didn't really know. She was shy, and she thought that part of her hometown would make her uncomfortable because she didn't know anyone.

She was wrong.

The faces she saw became friends, and after graduation, she stayed on as program director for the center because she felt so moved by what the center was doing—and by what she could do to help.

The center fed the poor, educated the young and old, and created a baseball league to keep the local kids off the streets and out of trouble. The center's mission gave her life meaning.

So many people looking for meaning in their lives find it by losing themselves in causes greater than they are.

Find one that inspires and touches you deeply. It could be anything from mentoring students to helping the homeless to finding the unemployed jobs.

It could lead to a new you.

YOU'RE THE ENGINEER

MARCH 4

Most of us start things and never finish them.

We just leave them lying around, promising to pick them up again when we get around to them. Then, our lives become so full of loose ends that we walk around in a perpetual tangle.

If you want to take purposeful action, rid yourself of this debris. Take a hard look at your unfinished projects and decide which ones will contribute to your vision and which ones are irrelevant.

Make the relevant ones a part of your goals, setting deadlines for completing them. Write off the irrelevant ones and move on to more meaningful activities.

We are like batteries. Sooner or later, we will lose all our energy. That's why it's essential to place your energy in something worthwhile.

"And what is a man without energy? Nothing—nothing at all."

Mark Twain said that more than a century ago. It is still true today.

THE POWER OF POSITIVE INFLUENCES

MARCH 5

Surround yourself with positive influences. When negative thinkers, images, or materials surround you, it is easy to get bogged down in hopelessness.

Read inspiring books and blogs. Listen to motivational podcasts and speakers. Attend positive-thinking seminars. And make it a point to read, watch, or listen to something positive and inspiring at least once every day.

Associate with positive people. Look for friends who feel good about themselves. People who need to tear down others are not happy with themselves and are not good for you or your attitude.

You end up being bitter at the world. Who needs that? How can you confront the negativity around you?

- **Think optimistically.** Be happy with your success and the success of others.
- **Smile.** You'll be surprised what that can do. Smile at others, and they'll smile at you.
- **Speak confidently.** Like a smile, confidence can be infectious.

See what happens if you try some of these tips. Your whole worldview can change.

FAKE IT TILL YOU FEEL IT

MARCH 6

S ome people blame themselves for everything negative that happens, even when they had nothing to do with it. They believe that somebody has to be blamed for everything, and, noble souls that they are, they step in and accept it.

Self-blame will send you on a guilt trip that compounds your depression and turns you into an Eeyore, the familiar donkey from *Winnie-the-Pooh* who views the world with a gloomy perspective.

Gretchen Rubin, author of *The Happiness Project*, found through her research and experience that people who act happier, friendlier, and more energetic will help themselves feel happier, friendlier, and more energetic.

It's the whole idea of "fake it until you feel it." Rubin says that works.

We all need to be built from the inside out. But sometimes, we create change from the outside in.

UPGRADE YOUR ESTIMATE

MARCH 7

S ome people dream exciting dreams, but never bring them out of dreamland. Often, the reason is that the person mistakes an exciting dream for an impossible dream.

There's an unconscious rating process that we go through when we're sizing up tasks. We think of the task in comparison to our own capacities.

If we think the task is bigger than we are, we become discouraged and we don't try.

If we think the task is beneath our capacities, we're bored by it, and we bypass it.

But if we think the task matches our capacities, we're likely to wade into it.

If the dream excites you, you can achieve it. If it were beyond your reach, it wouldn't excite you. So when you face a major challenge, give your estimate of your capabilities an upward revision.

The key to motivating yourself is to upgrade your estimate of your own capacities.

YOU CAN LIVE EVERY DAY OF YOUR LIFE

MARCH 8

The law of inertia holds that a body at rest tends to remain at rest, and a body in motion tends to remain in motion—at the same speed and in the same direction—unless acted upon by an outside force.

With one major difference, that law applies very well to the pattern of our lives.

- ❁ People who are successful tend to remain successful.
- ❁ People who are happy tend to remain happy.
- ❁ People who are respected tend to remain respected.
- ❁ People who reach their goals tend to go on reaching their goals.

So what's the major difference?

In physics, inertia is controlled by outside forces. But the real changes in the directions of our lives come from inside us.

As American philosopher William James said, "The greatest discovery of my generation is that man can alter his life simply by altering his attitude of mind."

You can live every day of your life. You can be alive to the tips of your fingers. You can accomplish virtually any worthwhile goal you set for yourself.

YOUR RESPONSE MATTERS

MARCH 9

Accidents of birth are beyond your control.

If you were born into a poor family without the means to send you to Harvard Business School or to MIT, you can't go back and trade in your parents for a set of millionaires.

If you were born with a physical disability, you can't trade in your body for a better model.

But remember that the cards you're dealt are less important than the way you play your hand. Circumstances may be beyond your control, but you have full control of your responses to those circumstances.

History books are full of success stories about people who focused their energies on the things they **could** do rather than the things they couldn't.

Adversity often leads to abundance. When things get tough, the tough get going.

ON THE WINGS OF IMAGERY

MARCH 10

Good writers and good speakers learn to paint pictures with words. A great poet provides an example.

Henry Wadsworth Longfellow was inspired by Paul Revere's mission. In his famous poem, he could have written, "Paul Revere rowed past the British warship, *Somerset*, on his way to Charles Town." But not Longfellow. He visualized the scene and translated his image into words for his classic poem, "Paul Revere's Ride":

> *A phantom ship, with each mast and spar*
> *Across the moon like a prison bar,*
> *And a huge black hulk, that was magnified*
> *By its own reflection in the tide.*

We can't all be Longfellows, but we can study the techniques and learn to translate the images and sounds we receive through our eyes and ears into words that will inform and inspire those who hear us.

Commit yourself today to connect with others at a deeper, more fulfilling level.

A VIRUS YOU DON'T WANT

MARCH 11

L ow self-esteem is like a low-grade virus. You're hardly aware that it's there. But it'll rob you of energy and your happiness. Jack Canfield, coauthor of the *Chicken Soup for the Soul* series, wrote this about low self-esteem:

"Build your self-esteem by recalling all the ways you have succeeded, and your brain will be filled with images of you making your achievements happen again and again. Give yourself permission to toot your own horn, and don't wait for anyone to praise you."

Thomas Carlyle lived more than a century before Canfield, and he worked as a teacher, a writer, a historian, and a mathematician, and was one of the most important social commentators of his time. He said, "Nothing builds self-esteem and self-confidence like accomplishment."

The years are different, but not the advice.

DON'T DANCE AROUND YOUR COMMITMENTS

MARCH 12

M any people go through life making decisions but dancing around their commitments. They're like the suitor who keeps saying over and over, "Oh yes, I'm going to marry you," but who refuses to set the date.

You see that played out in the popular movie *Runaway Bride.* Maggie, portrayed by actress Julia Roberts, constantly has cold feet at the altar, so much so that a reporter named Ike Graham comes to do a story on her.

In the process, he falls in love. Again, Maggie has cold feet. But not Ike. In a classic line from the movie, he says, "Look, I guarantee there'll be tough times. I guarantee that at some point, one or both of us is gonna want to get out of this thing. But I also guarantee that if I don't ask you to be mine, I'll regret it for the rest of my life, because I know, in my heart, you're the only one for me."

Ike Graham, portrayed by actor Richard Gere, knew that life is too important to be approached without commitment.

If you want to control your destiny, you must be willing to make a decision on what you want and to make a commitment to achieve it.

GO WHERE THE ACTION IS GOING TO BE

MARCH 13

A reporter once asked hockey great Wayne Gretzky why he always seemed to be where the puck was. Gretzky had a quick reply. "I always go to where the puck is going to be," he said.

In any pursuit, successful people are those who go where the action is going to be. They look down the road five years or more and ask the questions all of us should:

- ❂ What kind of person do I want to be?
- ❂ What assets will it take to get me there?
- ❂ How will I go about acquiring those assets?

These are vital questions that'll help you map out plans to get your goals from your head onto a tangible path to make it all happen.

If you keep your eye on where you are now, you'll never move forward. The possibilities lie in the future, and smart people try to put themselves where they are going to be.

That's how possibilities become realities; that's how you make contact with the puck of success.

IT TAKES TIME

MARCH 14

This is the age of instant everything. Somebody gave it a name—the "microwave society." Clever writers and producers of a television show can solve the most complicated dilemmas within thirty minutes, or an hour at most.

People are impatient and look for quick answers. But most of the things that make life worth living require time to develop. They don't come about quickly or easily or happen automatically.

Practical dreamers know that the harder they work, the luckier they get. Some of the best ideas need to incubate before they turn into successes.

CHOOSE YOUR BATTLE SITE
MARCH 15

Good generals know that the secret to winning wars is to pick your battle sites. Revolutionary War general Nathanael Greene knew.

In the winter of 1781, Greene retreated from a stronger British army under Lord Cornwallis. Greene crossed the Dan River in southern Virginia and waited for reinforcements. When he had them, he engaged Cornwallis in a battle in central North Carolina, near a place called Guilford Courthouse, more than two hundred years ago.

Greene chose that spot inside present-day Greensboro because of its familiarity, its high ground, and its easy access to a safe retreat.

On March 15, 1781, Greene lost the battle. But really, he helped win the Revolutionary War. Cornwallis lost nearly a quarter of his army in that battle, and by October of that year, the British surrendered. The Americans had won.

Greene can teach us much in business—and in life.

Find favorable terrain. Avoid head-on confrontations. That doesn't mean giving up. It means directing your efforts toward the situations you can influence and not wasting your energy on things that are beyond your control or things that don't really matter.

LOOK THEM IN THE EYE

MARCH 16

A Baptist minister in Moscow once told an American reporter an interesting story about the Russian poet Yevgeny Yevtushenko.

While visiting a wealthy American, the poet noticed a magnificent moose head mounted on the wall of the home.

"How could you bear to shoot such a magnificent animal?" Yevtushenko asked.

"It was easy," said his host. "He didn't look me in the eye. If he had looked me in the eye, I couldn't have shot him."

When you look people in the eye, they become more than passing acquaintances. They become people with whom you interact, if only briefly.

When speaking to anyone, whether it's your mother or an audience of thousands, try to establish eye contact. If you don't, your listeners may tune you out.

Practice it today with everyone you meet.

TO DREAM IS TO BE

MARCH 17

In the fabled kingdom of "what if," you'll find a blank check.

It is drawn on a limitless bank account, and a loving benefactor who can give you anything you want signs it. All you have to do is fill in your name on the blank line marked "pay to the order of."

So go ahead. Mentally write your name as the payee of the check. Now, in the "amount" space, write what you'd like most to have in life.

Go ahead. Reach for a star.

That blank check is what you write when you create a vision. A vision is a glowing mental picture of what your future will be. Create the vision and it will draw you toward its fulfillment. Or would you rather

- ☼ just muddle aimlessly through life?
- ☼ allow circumstances, or other people, to dictate the way you will spend the remainder of your life?
- ☼ fly by the seat of your pants, not taking the time to make the big decisions that could shape your life as you want it to be?

Of course not.

What do you want to be? Go for it.

FIX THE ROOF

MARCH 18

There's a marked difference between what's urgent and what's important.

An important task is something that moves you toward your goal. An urgent task may not be very important in the long run, but it demands immediate attention.

If the roof is leaking and water is dripping on your valuable armoire, the urgent task is to move the furniture. Moving the armoire doesn't solve your problem, and it doesn't move you toward your goal of a weather-tight house. But if you don't move it, serious consequences occur.

But in the long run? Fix the roof. That is the important task.

Think of your important tasks today that will help you reach your own personal goals. You know it's more than moving an armoire.

SOUL VACATION
MARCH 19

For the first three days of the expedition, the natives on an African safari carried the heavy bundles with no questions asked. On the fourth day, they simply refused to budge. Asked why, their leader explained that they were not being stubborn or lazy.

"For three days they have hurried through the jungle," he said. "This day, they must wait and let their souls catch up with their bodies."

We all need that time, at various stages of a busy day, to pause and get in touch with God, with ourselves, and with the deep, underlying purposes for which we labor.

We need to let our souls catch up with our bodies. Essayist Tim Kreider understands that. In June 2012, he wrote in the *New York Times*:

> The space and quiet that idleness provides is a necessary condition for standing back from life and seeing it whole, for making unexpected connections and waiting for the wild summer lightning strikes of inspiration—it is, paradoxically, necessary to getting any work done.

Take a recess today to reassess. It's good for the soul.

HOW TO LIVE YOUR BEST LIFE

MARCH 20

The microcosm of philanthropy is to give, not in the spirit of obligation or debt, but merely in the spirit of service.

Parents understand this concept innately because of the way they love their children. It's not that the child loves first and deserves to be loved in return, but simply because it's natural for parents to give unconditional love.

Philanthropy is much the same. To give back out of obligation is to miss the point and the blessing of the process. From the original Greek word *philanthropia*, the word *philos* means friend, while the word *anthropos* refers to mankind.

Living by a code of consistent giving equates to a life of significance and an attitude of gratitude.

From philanthropy comes the concept of stewardship in which we commit financial, educational, and other resources to nurture, nourish, guide, and grow both other people and their causes.

This investment of giving of one's self and sharing resources is central to the premise of stewardship. It is not limited by money, but only by one's heart, attitude, and commitment to effect lasting change.

God has blessed us. We have been given many opportunities. However, significance is measured not by our opportunities, but by our choices. Let us choose significance; let us all choose to give, not to merely give back.

After all, life is lived best when giving is seen not as an obligation, but as a privilege and a priority.

DON'T BE GUS

MARCH 21

Don't make statements you can't back up with facts.

Think of salespeople. They don't expect their clients to accept at face value everything they say. They are always prepared to prove every claim they make—and back it up with hard data, test results, and performance records.

Do that always, always, always.

In business, be sure the proof is authentic. And be sure you're not like Gus.

Gus sold homes, and he liked to demonstrate the sturdiness of his product by slamming his fist into the walls.

He knew—or thought he knew—where all the studs were, so his fist would strike solid wall. But on one new model, he miscalculated the location of the studs twice. He lost both home sales and had two ugly holes in a wall. Moreover, Gus ended up at home, soaking his fist in a pail of ice water.

Gus learned his lesson. Make sure you have the facts before you act.

DON'T SETTLE

MARCH 22

The winners in this world have always been those who have relentlessly used their freedom to choose how they would respond to whatever circumstances greeted them. For example:

- ❁ Colonel Harland Sanders, who began franchising Kentucky Fried Chicken at age sixty-five, was "too old" to start a business.
- ❁ Florence Chadwick knew that others had died trying to cross the English Channel.
- ❁ Steve Jobs got fired from the Apple, the company he first started in his garage.

We know what happened when these people decided to transcend their circumstances.

The world is still smacking its lips over Colonel Sanders's "finger-lickin' good" chicken, and in 1951, Florence Chadwick became the first woman to swim the English Channel—both ways.

Steve Jobs eventually went back to Apple and helped turn it into the world's largest technology company, creating products that have transformed millions of lives. He said, "Your work is going to fill a large part of your life, and the only way to be truly satisfied is to do what you believe is great work. And the only way to do great work is to love what you do. If you haven't found it yet, keep looking. Don't settle."

So don't let circumstances defeat you. Go out and create new circumstances.

LEAVE THE PAST BEHIND

MARCH 23

T hings that happened in the past are beyond your control. Forget about them and focus your efforts on the future.

If you introduced a product or service that bombed, you can't go back and un-introduce it. Start thinking about what you can do in the future to make up for the failure.

If you followed a hot tip on the stock market and got burned badly, you can't breathe life back into the worthless stock.

Learn from the experience and move forward.

The past may be a good place to visit, but it is a lousy place to live.

A RED-LETTER DAY

MARCH 24

S ome of the greatest success stories of history have followed a word of encouragement or an act of confidence by a loved one or a trusting friend.

For example, you may not know Sophia. But you may know her husband. He could write and Sophia knew it. But he was a heartbroken man.

When he went home to tell Sophia that he had been fired from his job in a customhouse and to confess that he was a failure, she surprised him with an exclamation of joy.

"Now," she said triumphantly, "you can write your book!"

"Yes," replied her husband despondently. "And what shall we live on while I am writing it?"

To his amazement, she opened a drawer and pulled out a substantial amount of money.

"Where on earth did you get that?" he exclaimed.

"I have always known that you were a man of genius," she answered. "I knew that someday you would write a masterpiece. So every week, out of the money you have given me for housekeeping, I have saved something; here is enough to last us for one whole year."

From her trust and confidence came one of the greatest novels in American literature, *The Scarlet Letter*.

By now, you may have guessed that Sophia's husband was Nathaniel Hawthorne.

So listen to the authentic voices of encouragement in your life.

Today is your day.

JUST SAY NO

MARCH 25

S ome people never realize their full potential simply because they don't recognize it. They go around with feelings of inferiority, assuming that everybody else knows more than they know or is more talented than they are.

Because they feel inferior, they hold back on expressing their ideas, and they fail to take the initiative. They believe others are better qualified to act, so they leave the action to others and don't view life through an optimistic lens.

This is a terrible waste of human talent. If you feel that way, it's time to take a positive look at yourself.

Everybody is good at something. If you can identify your special talent, then you can maximize your contribution to yourself, your company, and your community.

The only thing that is holding you back is you.

LISTEN TO THE "BIG SELF"

MARCH 26

You are always the best person to know what you can—or can't—do. It's that person inside you, or your "Big Self."

As you respond positively to that inner person who longs to control your life, you will find that self-confidence grows automatically.

The secret is in making the right choices. Refuse to be bound by perceived limitations.

At first, those choices might be a little hard to make. You might even have to fail sometimes to find out how to choose more effectively. But that's okay.

Consider what author J. K. Rowling said to a crowd of college graduates recently: "Some failure in life is inevitable. It is impossible to live without failing at something, unless you live so cautiously that you might as well not have lived at all—in which case, you fail by default."

It's better to try to do something and fail than to try nothing and succeed. And as you try more and more, you can learn more about your strengths and limitations.

Only then do the right choices become easier and more natural.

CELEBRATE NEW BEGINNINGS
MARCH 27

O n Easter Sunday, Dick Newsom will clean the tombstones of his parents, and they will both gleam as white as bleached whalebone in one of North Carolina's most sacred places, God's Acre in Winston-Salem.

It's a family tradition to spend every Easter at the historic Moravian cemetery. Newsom's parents were Moravian. And he raised his own family in the shadow of Moravians, singing, praying, and eating breakfast at his parents' church a few hours before every Easter sunrise.

He has a reason to be thankful. His son, Mark, is alive, a brain cancer survivor with a C-shaped scar on his bald head. When people ask about his scar, Mark has a ready answer, "The C stands for Christ."

Mark once worked for a big telecommunications company. Now, he runs a nonprofit, TriadBeHeadStrong, which helps brain cancer patients and their caregivers with the costs of medication, accommodations, and chemotherapy.

The gathering on Easter Sunday seems appropriate for the Newsom family.

It's a family tradition. But Easter also celebrates the resurrection of Jesus Christ, and people see Easter as a chance to start anew and remember what is important.

Like cleaning tombstones. Being with family. Being alive. Being Christlike.

LISTEN TO UNDERSTAND

MARCH 28

Effective listening means fewer errors and less wasted time.

But it's bigger than that. Listening builds friendships and careers. It saves money and marriages. And in our high-tech world, where we have become more solitary than ever, being a good listener helps you become more empathetic as you begin to understand.

You don't have to agree with the thoughts and feelings you hear. But if you are to deal positively with them, you must understand them. Once you acquire this understanding, you are in a better position to persuade people to take the action you want them to take.

But how do you do that? Here are five tips:

1. Come with an open mind.
2. Listen 75 percent of the time; speak 25 percent of the time.
3. Be respectful.
4. Don't multitask when you listen. Give all of your attention.
5. Show understanding. Ask questions and restate their point.

See what it can do for you. Think of what it did for former news anchor Diane Sawyer: "I think one lesson that I've learned is that there is no substitute for paying attention."

ONE MORE SENTENCE

MARCH 29

A great writer once confessed that the most daunting thing for him is a blank piece of paper in the typewriter.

So he developed a plan to get past the problem.

Each day, when he was ready to quit writing, he would leave a piece of paper in the typewriter with a sentence half-finished on it.

The next morning, the first thing he would do was to finish that sentence. Soon he would be thoroughly engrossed in his writing, and he was off to another productive day.

A to-do list, an assignment neatly stacked on your desk, or a time schedule will serve the same purpose.

Confusion is one of the greatest hindrances to action, so it always helps to know what you are going to tackle next as soon as you finish every task.

A WISE WARRIOR

MARCH 30

Before surrendering to the Europeanization of the continent, the American Indian was a keen observer because life and livelihood depended on close observation. Crowfoot, the Blackfoot warrior and orator, used poignant imagery derived from close observation in his memorable last words: "What is life? It is the flash of a firefly in the night. It is the breath of a buffalo in the wintertime. It is the little shadow that runs across the grass and loses itself in the sunset."

Someone who looks at his world closely and sees its vivid details uses that kind of imagery.

Great communicators like Crowfoot are good observers. They see the world up close, drink in its details, and describe them vividly to their audiences.

Commit today to taking in your surroundings and appreciating the beauty of your world.

TODAY IS...

MARCH 31

Mike seemed to have a knack for making each moment special, and every time he saw his friends, he'd say, "This is the best day of my life!"

His friends, though, were always skeptical.

"How can every day be the best day of your life?" they'd ask.

"This is the day that I am **alive**," he'd respond, smiling.

Mike died several years ago, but his reward is an eternity in which he saw every day as the best day of his life.

Today is the only day in which you can enjoy life, do good, and achieve success.

Yesterday is history.

Tomorrow is beyond your reach.

Today is yours to do with what you wish. It's the best day of your life.

Make the most of it. Be like Mike.

APRIL

SCALING YOUR OWN DAWN WALL

APRIL 1

You may remember Tommy Caldwell and Kevin Jorgeson.

These two climbers trained for more than five years to scale the largest granite monolith in the world—El Capitan's Dawn Wall in California's Yosemite National Park.

It's three thousand feet straight up, and they used nothing except their fingers, feet, and safety rope. They slept, recuperated, sipped whiskey, and ate canned peaches on the side of a sheer granite wall.

It took them nineteen days. They reached the top January 14, 2015.

Haphazard efforts didn't get Caldwell and Jorgenson there. They worked at it, and they had tried before—and failed. But they never stopped training. Scaling the Dawn Wall was their goal, their dream.

We all have our own Dawn Wall, and to achieve a significant accomplishment, you must be organized, untangling the tasks that confront you daily in order to focus on what is significant.

It takes work. Establish priorities and ask yourself, "What needs to be done next if I am to move closer toward my goal?"

If an activity is important to your goals, do it. If it's not, forget it and move on. Focus on what is significant to achieve your dream.

Caldwell and Jorgeson did. As Jorgeson tweeted, "To anyone writing about #dawnwall, this is not an effort to 'conquer.' It's about realizing a dream."

CONFIDENCE 101

APRIL 2

O ur emotions are our least dependable, and often our most deceptive, sensing devices. What the wise old masters have told us in a thousand ways boils down to this: it is easier to act your way into feeling the way you want than it is to feel your way into acting the way you want.

In other words, master your feelings; don't let them master you.

YOUR OWN PERSONAL LIST
APRIL 3

A list for you to think about today:

- ✪ Leave every person feeling better for having talked to you—they'll be happy to see you next time.
- ✪ Say what you mean, precisely what you mean, and only what you mean.
- ✪ When you're thinking ahead during a conversation, you can't hear what's being said.
- ✪ Listen at least twice as much as you talk—others will hear twice as much of what you say.
- ✪ Remember: we learn the most from our enemies.
- ✪ Talking when nobody is listening is as futile as trying to cut paper with half a pair of scissors.
- ✪ Personal communication is hindered by hasty assumptions.
- ✪ Self-centered people tend to monopolize the talking; secure people tend to monopolize the listening.
- ✪ You're wasting your time when you try to answer questions people are not asking.
- ✪ A "monologue in duet" happens when I'm thinking of what I'm going to say next while you're saying what you thought up while I was talking.
- ✪ The key to your success is to be sensitive enough to understand what other people want and generous enough to help them get it.
- ✪ Pay attention to others and they will pay attention to you.
- ✪ Be interesting by being interested.

OUR CYCLE OF LIFE

APRIL 4

F rom the poet T. S. Eliot, here are words to live by.

> *We must not cease from exploration*
> *And the end of all our exploring*
> *Will be to arrive where we started*
> *And know the place for the first time.*

Think of it this way: You work all year, saving money for the vacation you want to take. Then, you take that week, two weeks, or three weeks at someplace you discovered on the Internet or through the advice of a friend.

You savor it, experience it, and really understand how satisfaction is not just in realizing a goal, but in anticipating it for months. After coming home, you realize how your own space is a welcome sight, and you begin to see everything around you in a new and refreshing light.

You begin a new cycle of life and start planning for your next vacation. Each cycle has a beginning and an end, but it's also a renewal. Look at your life that way. The achievement of your vision is a rewarding vacation that you've planned and worked hard to achieve. Enjoy it. Celebrate it. Cherish the memory. But don't regard it as an end.

See it this way: it's a new beginning. We all need that.

OUR INVINCIBLE SURMISE

APRIL 5

The spiritual dimension is one that touches the core of your being. You gain access to it through the intuitive right side of the brain.

When you have spiritual balance, you are open to inspiration—that mysterious source of creativity that has been behind every great accomplishment. The renowned behaviorist Carl Jung said, "The great decisions of human life have, as a rule, far more to do with the instincts and other mysterious unconscious factors than with conscious will and well-meaning reasonableness."

George Santayana, the Spanish-born writer and philosopher, captured the thought in the following poem "O World, thou choosest not the better part."

> *O World, thou choosest not the better part!*
> *It is not wisdom to be only wise,*
> *And on the inward vision close the eyes,*
> *But it is wisdom to believe the heart.*
> *Columbus found a world, and had no chart,*
> *Save one that faith deciphered in the skies;*
> *To trust the soul's invincible surmise*
> *Was all his science and his only art.*

Columbus relied on his faith to discover America. He didn't know where he was going when he started out, and he sure didn't know where he was when he got there. But he followed what Santayana called his "invincible surmise" to become an indelible part of our history.

We all can do that—"trust the soul's invincible surmise."

THE MONEY IN YOUR POCKET

APRIL 6

Think about how you live.

If you live paycheck to paycheck, you're relying solely on income from wages, salaries, and commissions. It's like a free-flowing stream that overflows its banks in rainy seasons and dries up in summer.

That's what is known as linear income.

People who always seem to have an adequate supply of funds rely on income from growth in equity, from investments they've made, and from long-term business commitments that produce revenue virtually automatically. Thus, they concentrate on creating wealth.

That's residual income. It's like a reservoir whose waters rise during rainy seasons, holding back the excess for future needs and regulating the outflow to prevent flooding.

If you rely on linear income, you must go out every day and create new income. It's like carrying water from a spring a bucketful at a time.

But if you develop residual income, you can live on the fruits of your past efforts. It's like having water piped into your home. To build up a healthy residual income, base your major decisions on their lifetime value.

Keep your eye on the long term. If you do, you won't have to recreate your income every year.

EMBRACING CONFLICT

APRIL 7

The history of humanity is full of conflicts. But not all conflict is destructive or bad. We all know difficulties arise when you are confronted with two or more conflicting options. These options may involve conflicting needs, desires, or values, and they can come about from all kinds of combinations with two positive or negative experiences, or a mixture of both.

You know it'll happen; you just don't know what it'll look like. But one thing is certain: decisions involving this kind of conflict can be reached more easily if you are focused on your vision and goals and if you have an action plan in place. You simply choose the option that will move you closer to your goal in harmony with your action plan.

Of course, you can always change your action plan to accommodate opportunities that will move you toward your goal more quickly and easily. This approach will help you look upon conflict not as a battle that must be won, but as a problem that must be solved.

Conflict can make a positive impact on your life only when it is viewed as an opportunity to create positive change, and creative solutions can be reached as a result.

A RECIPE YOU NEED

APRIL 8

Our lives are the products of our decisions. If we make good decisions, we'll prosper. So how can we be sure that we're making good decisions?

Think of it like making a casserole. You find a good recipe and you follow it. Just as haphazard procedures won't guarantee good casseroles, haphazard decisions won't guarantee that you'll reach your goals in life.

May this recipe work for you:

- ⚙ **Identify the issue.** Be your own detective. Look, talk, research.
- ⚙ **Analyze the issue.** Ask yourself questions. Why is this necessary? If I **don't** make a decision, what happens? What if I do? What stands in the way? Then, rank them.
- ⚙ **Generate alternatives.** Brainstorm with others and look at the obstacles one at a time. Write down possible ways to remove them.
- ⚙ **Make a choice.** Answer the big questions: Will this work? And what will happen?
- ⚙ **Implement and Evaluate.** Did it work? Review your process yourself and ask to other people for their advice.

If you follow these procedures, you will continually learn from your mistakes, build on your successes, and determine how to measure your progress.

Then, when you achieve the future you planned for, savor the moment.

THE HEART OF COMMUNICATION

APRIL 9

L anguage is the primary way we convey thoughts and ideas. It turns abstract concepts into words that symbolize those thoughts. If the mind can immediately translate the sound of our voices and our words into mental pictures, communication becomes much more vivid and meaningful. The more skillful you become at conveying images, the more effective you will be as a communicator.

Leaders in the twenty-first century must take the initiative in breathing the soul of meaning and understanding into a body of data, thereby uniting a diverse workforce behind a common vision and goals. They must teach the people they lead to communicate through all levels of an organization.

Remember, all communication is personal. A speech, broadcast, or piece of writing—no matter how polished and professional—will not have a measurable effect unless it connects with the minds of the individuals hearing the message.

It's like a radio signal beamed at a certain frequency. If no radio receiver is tuned to that frequency, the signal vanishes into thin air.

FOLLOWING SISTER CEIL

APRIL 10

Many people carve out successful careers, reach financial security, and then look upon retirement as a yawning void. It need not be. Many people have discovered the secret of redirection in retirement.

Cecilia Harriendorf did.

For thirty years, Harriendorf worked as a TV producer. When she retired, she wanted to do more. She started as a religious teacher, earned a master's degree in theology, and became a religious education director.

Then, she spent a day at a convent. Her heart stirred. At age fifty-seven, she realized she wanted to become a nun. At age sixty-four, she achieved her goal and became Sister Ceil.

Like Sister Ceil, anyone can find new and stimulating channels in which to direct their creative energies. It may be in volunteer work, in charitable activities, or in totally new careers.

Today's young people can look forward to reinventing themselves many times through a progression of careers that could be as many as forty-five jobs in their lifetime. Older people can take advantage of the same environment.

When your bed has been made, and you're not yet ready to lie in it, look around for another exciting challenge.

It's out there. Go find it. Sister Ceil did. Her advice: Take a class. Read up on a topic. Talk to people. Talk to yourself.

"Take some time—walk or meditate—to really evaluate your next step," said Sister Ceil. "It's healthy and holy to step back and reflect upon your life and career."

YOUR A-LIST

APRIL 11

S uccessful people set goals, then devise strategies to help achieve them. Here's a logical process for moving toward your goals:

- ❂ Make a list of the things you need to do **immediately**, and then add daily and weekly tasks that move you toward your goals.
- ❂ Arrange these tasks in the order of priority. Address them one at a time.
- ❂ As you accomplish each task, cross it off your list.

If you can't do everything on the list, don't be discouraged. Put the unfinished items on your next to-do list and repeat the process.

When you learn to plan your time around priorities, you will find yourself moving effectively toward your desired future. Goal setting creates expectancy, and moving actively toward your goals delivers an energizing sense of accomplishment.

As you compile your list of priorities and move steadily through them, you are able to observe and measure your progress. This visible progress will give you a sense of deep satisfaction and the emotional energy to move on to even greater accomplishments.

A SECRET YOU NEED

APRIL 12

Some of the most disorganized people in the world are among the hardest workers. They work like crazy all day, conscientiously try to get everything done, and leave their offices tense because of important letters unwritten, people unseen, and urgent projects unfinished.

One reason they work longer and harder than everyone else is that they reinvent the wheel every time they need a ride.

They put forth extra effort because they do everything in a haphazard way, and often justify their disorganization on the grounds that they like their freedom to do things the way they want to do them.

But organization itself can be liberating by giving you more time to do the important things. The secret lies in focusing on the important—those things you need to do to move you toward your goal.

Clean your desk and your life of all the clutter it has collected—not by putting it all in the trash can, but by getting today's work done today.

YOU AND YOUR D.A.

APRIL 13

American poet Ralph Waldo Emerson wrote this:

> If a man has good corn, or wood, or boards, or pigs, to sell, or can make better chairs or knives, or crucibles or church organs than anybody else, you will find a broad, hard-beaten road to his house, though it be located in the woods.

That may have been true in the nineteenth century when Emerson wrote it. But today, being good at anything is no longer enough. Being good gets you into the arena, but it doesn't make you a winner.

To win, you need something extra that sets you apart from everyone else—something that makes people think of you first when they need what you offer. You **can't** simply compete on your strengths or simply being good. You have to compete with your differences—or that something extra—to prepare you for what the world will become.

That something involves your **differential advantage**—your D.A.

Your D.A. may come from doing things faster, cheaper, more skillfully, or more thoroughly than anyone else. It may come from having more experience, more specific knowledge, or in the sake of business, more convenient locations. It may come from being the biggest, the most flexible, or the most accessible.

Whatever it is, find it and exploit it. Your D.A. is your ticket to excellence.

THE IMPORTANCE OF FEELING AT HOME

APRIL 14

The people who work for a company need to have the same sense of belonging as do people who live in a community. A business organization is, after all, a community of people working toward common objectives.

In a healthy work environment, people feel loyalty toward the company akin to the loyalty they feel toward their hometowns or their alma maters. This feeling of community in the workplace should be one of the factors you look for when choosing a place to work.

This loyalty toward the company will serve you well in the team environment that is becoming the norm for progressive business organizations. It will help you to see things from the company's perspective and not just from the vantage point of your workstation.

But loyalty can have long-term effects as well. It can lead to relationships that build trust among your coworkers and help you network far beyond your workstation.

In our global economy, people change jobs more than they ever have, and research shows that many factors have caused employee loyalty to erode.

But take heart. Leaders and hiring managers who have created a progressive work environment tell the truth, communicate well, and value real-people relationships. Success follows. Loyalty too. Loyalty is timeless.

"The scholar does not consider gold and jade to be precious treasures," Confucius once said, "but loyalty and good faith."

THE PROFESSIONAL MENTALITY YOU NEED

APRIL 15

A re you a professional or a worker?

Before you answer, stop for a second and think about the world around you.

Workers see their jobs as necessary evils that must be endured until quitting time sets them free to pursue their **real lives**. Professionals see their careers as rewarding **components** of their real lives. They learn to integrate careers and their personal lives so that one meshes with and supports the other.

Workers wait for someone to tell them what to do and how to do it, and they let others worry about whether the way they're told to do it is the right way. They may concentrate on performing their assigned tasks well, but they won't worry about what happens outside their own areas.

Professionals are different.

They take responsibility for their own success and for the success of their organizations. They are constantly looking for things that they personally can do to contribute to organizational success.

Whether you're a professional or a worker doesn't depend on your job description. It depends on your attitude toward the job and the company.

So think like a professional. You'll benefit your company, your community, and yourself.

LEARNING FROM YOUR WRONG NOTES

APRIL 16

We all make mistakes, act foolishly, or make bad decisions at times. But we don't have to be stuck with them for the rest of our lives.

We may have to accept the consequences—and the consequences may not be pleasant. But the achievers among us refuse to become prisoners of our mistakes. We know that the past is beyond our control, so we focus our efforts on the future.

But it doesn't end there. People gain wisdom when they seek to learn something of value from each mistake or failure rather than measuring them by their immediate consequences. Instead, they measure their mistakes or failures against their long-term goals and their inherent worth as human beings. People who do that will regard their setbacks as minor and their opportunities as major.

When they fail, they find out what led to the failure. Then they congratulate themselves on the lesson they've learned and resolve not to go down that path again.

So listen to the advice of American essayist John Burroughs who said, "Keep moving."

Or better yet, listen to one of the most talented people to climb behind a keyboard, Dave Brubeck, who said, "There's a way of playing safe, there's a way of using tricks, and there's the way I like to play, which is dangerously where you're going to take a chance on making mistakes in order to create something you haven't created before."

Mistakes are like wrong notes. Learn from them. You'll find the melody.

BUILDING YOUR BRAND

APRIL 17

W hen you think of Apple, you think of iPhones, iPads, and Steve Jobs. With Hershey's, you immediately think of chocolate, and when you think of CNN, you think TV news.

What do people think of when they hear your name? If you have properly positioned yourself, they should think of all the things you stand for—the things that you do better or differently than what anybody else does.

Positioning is the journey to acquiring your personal brand and includes all the things you must do to get people to think of you first and do business with you.

But branding is the destination. It is the result of effective and consistent positioning. Both must be handled with mastery through marketing, sales, and promotion.

As a result of knowing you or doing business with you, people should have confidence that they will benefit in a very valuable way. This value must not be based on the way you define it, but on the way others interpret it.

Your value is always measured by the size of the problems you're capable of solving. So make it your purpose today to achieve a personal brand that stands for value.

THREE THINGS TO REMEMBER

APRIL 18

H ere are three principles to keep in mind as you work toward creating a better you:

- ✪ **Extend genuine value.** Value is not something that **you** consider to be value, but results that your clients consider to be valuable.

- ✪ **Be authentic.** Authenticity is better than charisma. While being charismatic and dynamic are wonderful traits, being authentic is being precisely what the world expects of you. Make sure that you are what you say you are.

- ✪ **Be a disciplined worker.** Figure out which parts of the day are creative hours for **you**, and use those hours to the fullest. This calls for discipline, especially if you're an entrepreneur with no boss to watch over you. Just remember the law of behavioral economics: every behavior you display must produce economic benefit.

Remember that your name is your brand, and your brand is your name. Guard your brand the way you guard your reputation. Do nothing that would deflate its value because in our age of social media, remember one thing: **Google never forgets.**

NO CLOTHESPINS ON MY NOSE, PLEASE

APRIL 19

I'd like to share two stories.

In 1999, a man from Iowa accomplished a mind-boggling feat: he built a freestanding house of standard playing cards 131 stories high, stacking 91,800 cards to a height of 25.29 feet.

In 2001, Gary Turner of Great Britain accomplished a feat of another dimension—he clipped 153 ordinary wooden clothespins to his face.

Both men were successful in accomplishing what they set out to accomplish. But was what they did significant?

Their feats weren't plastered on front pages worldwide and won't be chronicled in history books a century hence. Their significance lies in the fact that they made the *Guinness Book of World Records*. But the Guinness book is largely a collection of trivia. If your greatest success is achieving mention in that volume, then you have not lived a life of significance.

Albert Einstein was on target when he advised, "Try not to become a man of success. Rather become a man of value."

That makes uncommon sense.

Truly happy people aim for significance, not just success. They're not interested in how many cards they can stack, one on the other, or how many clothespins they can attach to their faces. They seek opportunities to wield their talents in such a way as to affect the world for the better.

HOW TO SOAR

APRIL 20

You see it in business, any business, no matter the size or profit margin: some workers accept a ceiling on success in return for a steady income.

They are not boat rockers, but believe in doing things the way they've always been done, which they perceive as the safe, cautious way.

They concentrate on the **means**. They do their jobs without worrying about how their jobs contribute to the total picture.

But others concentrate on the **ends**. They see their jobs in terms of how they contribute to the organization's success.

They are usually perceived as excellent employees because they go the extra mile. They keep up with the latest developments in their field, share knowledge with others, and exude confidence—dressing and grooming themselves for success, conscious of the importance of image.

If that describes you, you will realize that your possibilities have no ceiling, and you can soar as high as your initiative and imagination will take you.

And you can take your company with you.

WHERE YOUR ATTENTION NEEDS TO BE

APRIL 21

When you sit down at your desk each morning, where is your attention focused? Is it on your plans for today, next week, next year, or the next ten years?

Elliott Jacques, who has a doctoral degree in social relations, says that hourly workers have an hour's or a day's time horizon. Supervisors have a week or a month's time horizon. Managers may have a year or five years.

Leaders, though, may have a twenty-five-year horizon.

To look ahead that far, leaders need to have a vision of the company's future: what will it look like ten or twenty-five years down the road?

Don't focus on present circumstances. Proactive planning shows an awareness of present circumstances, but it transcends to creating new circumstances.

Don't dwell on the past. It's no longer a reliable guide to the future. The world is changing too fast, and business and commerce no longer follow the channels of the past.

Today's leaders must be willing to carve new channels, create new structures, and thereby control the future.

So can you.

WHAT MEANS MORE THAN MONEY?

APRIL 22

Building value involves far more than building a large, sustainable income. To be truly successful and significant, you must regard income as a means to an end—your service to humanity.

Your worth as an individual bears only a marginal relationship to your personal income.

Our country's president earns far less in salary than real estate developer Donald Trump's estimated sixty million dollars a year. Yet the president's value as the leader of the world's most powerful nation outweighs Trump's value.

A teacher's earnings are quite modest compared to the earnings of, say, a celebrity like Kim Kardashian. Yet his or her contributions toward an orderly and prosperous society are incomparably higher.

You build value in yourself by earning a reputation for putting quality and integrity into everything you do.

Your value grows as you use your success, not just to feather your own nest but also to serve others. When you put service to humanity first, self-sufficiency for yourself follows naturally.

In the words of King David, "I was young and now I am old, yet I have never seen the righteous forsaken or their children begging bread."

Build value into everything you do and you will prosper materially, emotionally, and spiritually.

ONE STEP AT A TIME
APRIL 23

You have this dream, but you don't know how to get there. Break it down and dissect it. Like diagraming a sentence, all you need is a structure to get there.

Here are some ideas:

- ❂ **Get sound advice.** Blind action gets you nowhere.
- ❂ **Lay the groundwork.** Study, research, and find equipment.
- ❂ **Stick to a timetable.** Set short-term goals. Write them down.
- ❂ **Don't do everything yourself.** Delegate. Sometimes, it's not all about you.
- ❂ **Look for small successes.** Those small successes lead to a pattern of success.
- ❂ **Concentrate on opportunities.** See them and take advantage.
- ❂ **Share your knowledge and expertise.** Help others and you'll help yourself.
- ❂ **Never approach a task tentatively.** Be bold. There is no turning back.
- ❂ **Think things through.** Examine and visualize before you start.
- ❂ **Clear the decks of unfinished things.** Set aside anything irrelevant.

Follow these steps for every dream you have, establish achievable goals, get help, and look for those **successes**, no matter how small. It'll happen. You'll see.

WATCH FOR DIRTY WATER

APRIL 24

Remember this acronym: GIN GO—garbage in, garbage out. I'm not so sure it applies to computers. I know it applies to us.

The ghosts of what we erase on a computer remain deep within the system, electronically etched into the hard drive. I'm told that computer experts can extract it long after it's been erased.

I don't know about those things, but I do know that what goes into the human mind can remain to contaminate it or to enrich it.

The mind is like a sponge. If you soak a sponge in dirty water and squeeze it, dirty water will come out. But if you then soak it in pure water and squeeze, you still get dirty water. Why? Some of that dirt stays.

When you fill your mind with unhealthy or unproductive thinking, it penetrates beyond the conscious mind and into the subconscious. There it stays. The subconscious doesn't forget. The garbage that comes into the mind will stay to influence future thoughts and actions the way that dirty water influences the pure water that pass through the sponge.

The things we see and hear become a part of us. They're the things we think about in moments of solitude. To become upright, successful, and significant leaders, it's necessary to fill our minds with thoughts and ideas that characterize upright, successful leaders.

USE YOUR FREEDOM OF CHOICE

APRIL 25

These days, we hear a lot about freedom. But we rarely exercise our most precious freedom.

You **won't** find it in the Bill of Rights, and if you read it, the Declaration of Independence only hints at it. No document of any nation anywhere in the world clearly spells it out. That's because no nation can give it to you, and no nation—no people—can take it away from you.

This freedom is equally available to all people regardless of race, religion, sex, economic status, or circumstance. It is available to the prisoner, the invalid, the poor, the victim of discrimination, the timid, even the person who lives under a repressive regime.

What is it? It's this: **each of us has the freedom to choose how we will respond to the circumstances in which we find ourselves.**

Life is a giant smorgasbord of choices. Yet here we stand, with our small plates that can hold only so much. Freedom demands that we make choices.

SYSTEMIZE YOUR NEW ROUTINE

APRIL 26

You can relieve yourself of unimportant tasks by systematizing as much of your routine work as possible. Here's how.

For example, if you have to write a lot of letters in response to inquiries, you can probably divide the inquiries into a few basic categories. Then, instead of having to compose a new letter for each individual inquiry, you can write a form letter for each category.

Stored in the cloud or in a folder on your computer, these letters can be used to answer nearly all of your inquiries.

A great deal of valuable time is wasted shuffling papers. So work out a system that gets you through a chore in short order and clears your desk for the truly important things.

When you receive a letter, read it and decide quickly whether you should handle it or refer it to someone else for action.

If it's something for someone else to handle, write appropriate notes on the letter and immediately send it to the person who will handle it.

If it's something you need to handle, take the appropriate action. Then, respond to all the mail you plan to answer, filing those letters you need to keep as you go and discarding those you have no reason to keep.

When you're finished, you're ready to tackle the important work.

FINDING YOUR PRACTICAL DREAM
APRIL 27

"The Impossible Dream" is a great and inspiring song from the musical *Man of La Mancha*. But it is a lousy way to spend your life. The better life lesson is this: do practical dreaming— dreaming possible dreams about what you do best.

Usually, the first stop in determining what you can do best is ruling out what you can do only poorly, or not at all. Then, you are free to concentrate all of your creative energies on your abilities and strengths.

People who continually push themselves furiously against their natural limitations tend to become frustrated and embittered. They rob the world of what they could do best because they spend their lives trying to do what they can do only poorly or not at all.

Constant failure beats them down, and they lose all semblance of self-confidence. Such people expend all their energies chasing what is really an impossible dream.

So go after what is practical: a dream that channels your passion. To find out what that is, ask yourself four questions:

1. Is it something you'd do for free?
2. When you're talking about it, do you become more enthusiastic?
3. If you could, would you spend more time doing it?
4. And when you do it, do you feel good about yourself and lose track of time?

Answer those questions, and you'll find your passion—and your practical dream.

BE THE ARROW

APRIL 28

Stress often gets a bad rap.

Good stress can be used like the tension in a bowstring. Unless you put stress on the bowstring, your arrow won't fly straight to its mark.

Stress can affect a person in the same way. Someone who is experiencing no stress is also experiencing no challenge, and people who are not challenged will not exert themselves to succeed.

In the end, they become bored and unmotivated.

Challenged students, though, are different. They're excited, ready for action, like a well-trained team going into a championship game. They have tension, like a bowstring, that puts an edge on their performance, causing them to play their best.

You should feel the same with your vision and your action plan. It should compel you to move toward your goals.

That's why it's important to create an exciting vision. An effective vision arouses your passions, and it sets in front of you a future so enticing that you can taste it.

See yourself in your vision. If you can't, it won't have drawing power. The key to motivation is identity.

If you can't identify personally with the vision and goals, you won't be able to generate enthusiasm and sufficient interest to make it happen.

But you can. Visualize it. Stress helps.

BUILDING YOUR PERSONAL CREDIBILITY

APRIL 29

Your personal credibility communicates a very important message to the people you deal with. People like to deal with competent people whom they can trust.

You build confidence in your competence by becoming good at what you do. Whatever your job is, make excellence the standard by which you judge your own performance. Become a student of your job, always looking for better ways of doing it.

Observe your coworkers who excel at their jobs, seek their advice, and follow their positive examples.

Sometimes your credibility depends on your willingness to say, "I can't." If someone makes a request that you can't fulfill, say so, and let the person know why. That's better than making a commitment you know you can't keep. If you promise something you can't deliver, the person you promised may go away happy. But that happiness will turn to anger as soon as the commitment is broken.

If you're asked to do something you can't do, say, "I can't do that." Then, try to suggest an alternative.

But when you're not sure you can, never say, "I'll do it."

You're likely to end up with a botched job and an angry individual.

LOOK FOR YOUR NICHE

APRIL 30

The surest route to success?

Find a highly profitable niche for which you are well qualified and give that specialized area everything you have.

But that's just the beginning.

Focus on your strongest natural abilities. Take a close look at what your education and experience best qualifies you to do. Look for those things that you know the most about and in which you demonstrate the most credibility to others.

The important point to remember is that, in any profession, you will usually be most productive doing those few things that you do best and most enjoy doing.

That's what Ben Cohen and Jerry Greenfield, his childhood friend, did.

Cohen taught pottery and made ice cream on the side. When he and Greenfield—a frustrated lab technician—reunited, they looked into going into the food business and chose ice cream.

They took a five-dollar course on ice-cream making and moved to Burlington, Vermont, because the college town didn't have an ice cream parlor. They opened one in 1978 in a converted gas station.

That was the birth of Ben & Jerry's Ice Cream.

In finding your most valuable niche, you have to balance what you can do best against what has the highest perceived value.

Cohen and Greenfield did. You can too.

MAY

A FRUITFUL SEARCH

MAY 1

Humans have that unique ability to make their lives better by building on the vast storehouse of wisdom and knowledge that has been transmitted from one generation to the next. A few minutes at a public library can reveal the wisdom of the philosophers, the romance of poets, or the knowledge of the scientists, even from centuries ago.

You don't have to reinvent the wheel, rediscover fire, or develop a language. It is humbling to realize that most of the products of our lifetime are possible only because of the work and creative genius of those who have gone before us.

A FRUITLESS SEARCH

MAY 2

One classic myth is that a person will find happiness at a future time in a magic moment—and usually in a distant place.

Yet, as psychiatrist Viktor Frankl said, "It is the very pursuit of happiness that thwarts happiness."

Those who spend their lives searching for happiness never find it, while those who search for meaning, purpose, and strong personal relationships find that happiness usually comes to them as a by-product of those three things.

IT TAKES WORK

MAY 3

In editing a book of early writings by Ernest Hemingway, William White, a journalism and English instructor, unearthed stories that Hemingway wrote between 1920 and 1924 when he was a reporter for a Toronto newspaper.

The writing was good. But it wasn't superb. It gave only a faint glimmer of the masterful storyteller who would emerge in *The Old Man and the Sea*.

What was lacking? Experience.

The genius was there all along, but it needed to incubate. The sands of time can abrade or polish, but you need to remember that it all depends on whether you use your time purposely or let it pass haphazardly.

Hemingway didn't transform himself into a successful novelist through one blinding flash of literary insight. Like most people, he progressed from good to superb through hundreds of tiny improvements.

Day to day.

And that goes with anything you do, anything you try.

You go through hundreds of tiny improvements to master a job, a skill, a relationship, and when you do, it'll remind you of something that philanthropist, businessman, and British hairdresser Vidal Sassoon who reportedly once said: "The only place where success comes before work is in the dictionary."

DEFINE YOUR PRINCIPLES

MAY 4

S uccessful people don't lie awake at night agonizing over decisions and directions. They simply consult their principles.

They make decisions that are in harmony with these principles, and they don't second-guess themselves and seldom reverse themselves.

You can do that too. You can choose the principles you want to guide you by first identifying the values you hold dear.

To do that, here are three simple steps:

- ✪ Think of the roles that are important to you in your family, vocational, community, and religious lives.
- ✪ Now think of the people, activities, and qualities you value in each role.
- ✪ For each value, write a supporting principle. Make it personal. State it in the form of a sentence describing yourself as you would like to be, in the light of these values. Do this for each of the roles that are important to you.

When you have identified the principles you want to guide your life, use them in measuring each possible choice. And when you have found a pursuit that conforms to your basic principles—while allowing you to do what you do best and enjoy most—you will have found your ideal calling.

A nice discovery. Now, go for it.

REDIRECT YOURSELF

MAY 5

The best way to avoid burnout is to learn the secret of redirection early in life. This option might mean pursuing some interest you've always put off because of work.

It might mean a career change, a change of residence, or learning a new skill. People who learn how to redirect often find that the spouse they had long neglected is the dream companion they have sought.

A person who has always been money oriented might discover new meaning by offering free community service.

Someone has said that the person who is successful in only one area of life is a failure. If you want to avoid burnout, keep reaching up and keep reaching out.

For some, it's not retirement they aspire to; it may be redirection instead.

REPEAT AFTER ME

MAY 6

The use of the present tense seems to add more certainty to the fulfillment of your goal because the subconscious mind accepts that goal as an accomplished **fact** and guides your behavior accordingly.

Say this out loud: "I feel more energetic because I have lost ten pounds."

Isn't that more convincing than saying, "I plan to gain more energy by losing ten pounds"?

Dave Phillips, North Carolina's former commerce secretary and former U.S. Ambassador to Estonia, had a pin that simply said one word: Attitude. He got it from his wife's uncle, and he wore it all the time when he promoted North Carolina to the world.

He now keeps it on his dresser because that pin with that one word—**Attitude**—made all the difference.

State your goals in the affirmative and in the present tense, and your subconscious will cause you to act in a way that is consistent with your goals.

Your future starts now.

YOU ON LIFE'S BATTLEFIELD

MAY 7

Y ou can guarantee that your life and your relationships with people will fall into one of three categories:

- ✪ Those you want to influence and can.
- ✪ Those you'd like to influence but can't.
- ✪ Those who are not worth influencing.

Think of it like triage, a system developed during warfare for classifying the wounded, from the ones who will survive to the ones who won't.

On the battlefield, the doctors working triage were bent on saving young, healthy bodies battered by bullets and bombs.

When it comes to relationships, conduct your own version of triage. Choose to focus your energies because every relationship can't be saved.

Consider the three points as action steps:

- ✪ Ignore the challenges that are unlikely to affect your success and happiness either way.
- ✪ Look for ways to adjust to those situations that you can do nothing about.
- ✪ Focus your efforts on the things you can change.

Start that **today** and see what happens.

BE TRUE TO YOURSELF

MAY 8

People without principles are like boats without rudders or cars without steering wheels. Their directions are aimless and their decisions haphazard.

When principles occupy the center of your life, they help you arrive quickly at the right decision for you when opportunities arise or crises loom.

When your life is centered on people, what's important is what others want. When it's centered on possessions, the important thing is what you have. When it's centered on activities, the important thing is what you do.

But when your life is centered on principles, you are being true to yourself.

Stephen Covey, author of the bestseller *The Seven Habits of Highly Effective People*, summed it up perfectly:

> You have to decide what your highest priorities are and have the courage—pleasantly, smilingly, nonapologetically, to say "no" to other things. And the way you do that is by having a bigger "yes" burning inside. The enemy of the "best" is often the "good."

ORDER THIS OMELET

MAY 9

Think of how people work.

In some places, salaried professionals look down their noses at hourly employees. They fail to recognize the levels of skill, intelligence, and diligence required to perform the basic tasks that keep us in business.

Professionals who take this attitude are closing their eyes and ears to a fertile source of excellent ideas.

The people who know the most about what customers want are the people who are in daily contact with them. The people who know best how to operate our equipment are the people who operate it daily. When management fails to recognize that, it's not the employees who are inferior—it's the management.

Any business, any organization must be able to talk to itself: its people must be taught to communicate with one another across functional and departmental lines and up and down the corporate ladder.

If not, a business or an organization is simply like a carton of eggs, with each unit enclosed in an individual shell, separated by barriers that keep them from rubbing together. To be successful, an organization has to be like an omelet, with the various units blending their talents and interests to produce a harmonious whole.

The ability to communicate effectively across functional and supervisory lines is one of the most crucial abilities in any organization, or any business in the twenty-first century.

THE PERILS OF SELF–IMPORTANCE

MAY 10

Self-importance leads to misery.

We all know athletes, celebrities, even members of our extended family who believe the world revolves around them. And according to the Reverend Billy Graham, the pitfalls of our American lifestyle are pride, lack of shame, and self-centered indulgence.

Find a self-centered person, and you'll see a person who is driven by a negative self-image. That leads to loneliness and fear, anger, and isolation.

Those are not ingredients for a successful life. Remember this verse from Philippians:

Do nothing out of selfish ambition or vain conceit. Rather, in humility value others above yourselves, not looking to your own interests but each of you to the interests of the others.

Only then will you truly grow.

BUILD YOUR FUTURE

MAY 11

You can't take charge of your life without an awareness of where you've been, where you are, and where you're going. But you have to remember you can't build your life on the past. The past is gone.

Nor can you allow your destiny to be limited by present circumstances. The present is fleeting.

The only place left to build your life is in the future. You can let the future happen, or you can create it. You create it by forming a clear, vivid picture of what you want and fixing your mental and emotional eyes on that picture. Let it become your vision, and it will draw you toward the fulfillment of your goals.

Start today with hope and anticipation.

YOGI'S WISDOM

MAY 12

Remember the fable of the golden goose?

The goose produced a golden egg each day, but that wasn't enough for the impatient owner. He decided to slaughter the goose and harvest all the eggs at once. The result: no more goose and no more eggs.

A tough lesson. But listen to poet-philosopher Ralph Waldo Emerson, who has some sound advice: "Adopt the pace of nature: her secret is patience."

Impatience is what causes people to give up on their goals before their efforts have had a chance to bear fruit. Patient people are much different.

They learn to distinguish between disasters and temporary setbacks and have come to realize patience is the balance between boldness and prudence, between rashness and wisdom.

When things don't work out, they ask "Why?" Then, they turn the "why" into "how" and begin developing strategies to convert the setback into a success.

When you develop your action plan for life, set realistic timetables. If the timetable you've set seems to be unrealistic, remember that most things take longer than you think they do. Recalculate, make your adjustments, and keep moving toward your goal.

Remember Yogi Berra's famous dictum, "It ain't over till it's over."

RESPECT EVERYONE

MAY 13

I t has been consistently demonstrated that if you treat people like winners, they'll act like winners. If you treat them like losers, they'll act like losers.

Eliza Doolittle, the character in the Broadway musical *My Fair Lady*, put it this way in speaking of the kindly Colonel Pickering: "The difference between a lady and a flower girl is not how she behaves, but how she is treated. I shall always be a common flower girl to Professor Higgins, because he always treats me as a common flower girl, and always will. But I know that I shall always be a lady to Colonel Pickering, because he always treats me like a lady, and always will."

Find something to respect about everyone you deal with.

People will instinctively seek to live up to your respect, and they'll treat you with respect too, making it easier for you to respect yourself and live up to their expectations.

See the good in others.

THE BLESSING OF GOOD COMPANIONSHIP

MAY 14

All of us need to feel that we're part of a group where we can relax and be ourselves. In the presence of like-minded friends, we can exchange pleasantries, talk shop, talk golf, talk books, or just keep silent if we want.

Your colleagues at work can be a fertile source of friendships of this type. But don't confine your friendships to the workplace. Cultivate friends in other walks of life. These friendships will broaden your perspective and open up new opportunities for growth.

Develop interests that have no direct connection with your job. Take up a hobby or a sport. Then seek out others who share your interest.

You'll soon begin to build a network of friendships that will prove valuable in ways you can't anticipate.

DON'T ROB YOU OF YOU

MAY 15

M any people live in a musty world of "gotta" and "oughta." They are always telling themselves or others that they've "gotta do" this or they "oughta do" that.

So, they live in a world of "should," and when they don't do what they feel they should do, they feel guilty. When others are told what they've "gotta do," they feel resentful. You need to avoid "gotta do" thinking.

But how do you do that? The answer is life management—looking further ahead and thinking of what you want to be and how you want to get there. Set the goals you want to achieve, and align your actions to attain them.

Comedian Jerry Seinfeld had a way to keep himself on track. He would write jokes every day, and to make sure he did that, he had a big calendar on the wall and marked a red X through a particular day to remind him to fulfill what he set out to do.

"Gotta do" thinking is simply another way to procrastinate. And procrastination has more to do with a "failure to do" than with what we actually do.

It robs you of money by stealing your time. But moreover, it robs you of you.

SEEK SMALL VICTORIES

MAY 16

There's nothing so demoralizing as constant failure. There's nothing so invigorating as repeated success.

That's why political candidates work hard to create bandwagon effects. They know that success breeds success. For example, look at the Iowa caucuses and the New Hampshire primary.

In 2014, Iowa ranked thirtieth among the fifty states in population, and New Hampshire ranked forty-second.

Neither state sends a large enough delegation to the national political conventions to make a significant difference.

Yet in every presidential election year, aspiring candidates brave the frigid winters of those two states, hoping to win the majority of delegates to the nominating conventions.

Why?

They hope that by winning in these two early contests, they can establish a pattern of success that will help carry them to victory in the larger states.

You can build momentum toward the big win by establishing a pattern of success. So seek small victories. Win enough of them, and you'll get used to winning. Then what will happen?

You'll be winning the big ones.

"YOU DID IT"

MAY 17

If you really want people to work their hearts out for you, follow the example of Bear Bryant, the great University of Alabama football coach.

Bryant brought an era of glory to the Crimson Tide, but he never hogged the credit. Bear once said, "If anything goes bad, I did it. If anything goes semi-good, then we did it. If anything goes real good, then you did it. That's all it takes to get people to win football games."

With this attitude, Bear Bryant became national coach of the year three times and Southeastern Conference coach of the year twelve times. He coached six national championship teams and retired from coaching with an astonishing 323 victories—at that time, the most victories of any coach in history.

But if he were still around, he would tell his University of Alabama players, "You did it."

THE LONG VIEW

MAY 18

I f you could view your life as you do a highway from an airliner, many of the detours and curves would make more sense.

The value of taking the long view of life is that it enables you to see problems as opportunities, passing up the fun-for-the-moment to pursue a worthwhile goal.

Leslie Dewan did just that.

She is in her early thirties, a Massachusetts native with a doctorate degree in nuclear engineering. She cofounded Transatomic Power. Its aim: to build a nuclear reactor fueled by nuclear waste.

For decades, nuclear waste has been seen as a huge problem. But Dewan saw it through the eyes of an entrepreneur, not those of a cynic.

And where did she find her idea of Transatomic? From stacks of old scientific papers she pored through when she was a PhD candidate at Massachusetts Institute of Technology.

She found them so driven, so hopeful. And by mining the past, Dewan found her life's purpose.

"We're going to take a technology that at the time had only been used for weapons," Dewan told *Esquire* magazine. "And we're going to use it to power the world."

A WRITER'S PERSONAL CREED

MAY 19

R obert Louis Stevenson, the author of the classic *Treasure Island*, had a personal creed that is full of wisdom and common sense:

- Make up your mind to be happy and learn to look for pleasure in little things.
- Do the best you can in your circumstances. The trick is to make the laughter outweigh the tears.
- Don't take yourself too seriously or think that you should be spared the misfortunes that befall others.
- You can't please everybody. Don't let criticism worry you.
- Don't let your neighbors set your standards. Be yourself.
- Do the things you enjoy.
- Avoid people who make you unhappy.
- Develop new interests.
- Don't harbor useless regrets. Don't spend your life brooding over sorrows and mistakes, and don't be the one who never gets over things.
- Do whatever you can for those less fortunate than you.
- Keep busy at something, for a busy person never has time to be unhappy.

CONSIDER THE SOURCE

MAY 20

I f you don't believe the messenger speaks louder than the message, consider these two statements:

1. "Ain't we got all the fools in town on our side? And ain't that a big enough majority in any town?"
2. "A majority can never replace one man… Just as a hundred fools do not make one wise man, a heroic decision is not likely to come from a hundred cowards."

Read them again. Maybe even one more time.

The first statement came from a book by Mark Twain; the second from one by Adolf Hitler.

The odium attached to the name of Adolf Hitler negates any positive element in anything he ever said, and no amount of eloquence will lend it respectability.

If you want to communicate in a positive way, you must cultivate a positive image as a person.

NEVER LET THEM SEE YOUR BRACES

MAY 21

During the first half of his life, Franklin Delano Roosevelt never slowed down. At age twenty-eight, he served in the New York State Senate, and while he was still in his early thirties, he was appointed assistant secretary of the navy. By thirty-eight, he was nominated for vice president of the United States.

By thirty-nine, he was stricken with polio. His legs were paralyzed. Roosevelt tried to regain his ability to walk through swimming, but for the rest of his life, he could stand only with the help of braces. Nevertheless, he led the nation through the Great Depression and World War II.

When Americans saw their president, they didn't see a handicapped man struggling to stay on his feet. They saw a jaunty president who was eager to lead, one who told his constituents that "the only thing we have to fear is fear itself."

Though physically challenged, Roosevelt never allowed himself to be perceived as a disadvantaged man. He exuded an aura of confidence and energy, qualities America needed to survive the economic crisis of the 1930s and to win the epic battle of the 1940s.

So, when you face adversity, never be fearful. Think of FDR. He never was.

STOCK UP ON ENDORPHINS

MAY 22

Your body has an internal source of self-esteem. It produces endorphins—a secretion that acts on the brain and produces that euphoric feeling you get when you're with just the right people in just the right circumstances. Exercise produces endorphins, which is why joggers often feel a high after exercising. The presence of people you love also stimulates endorphin production.

Another thing that generates endorphins is hugs.

The next time you hug someone you love, notice the warm, upbeat feeling it gives you. If you're not in the habit of hugging your children, your spouse, or your significant other, take up the habit. Make it a warm, cheek-to-cheek, loving embrace.

It will make you—and your hugging partner—feel better.

LOOK FOR LOFTIER PEAKS

MAY 23

M any couples have a vision of home, career, and a family of happy, healthy children. Through hard work and ingenuity, they achieve everything they seek.

Then one day, they realize that the home is paid for, the children are educated and have successful families of their own, their retirement nest egg is substantial and secure—and they have nothing left to live for.

The tragedy is that many such people equate the achievement of their vision with the end of their life's mission.

Nothing could be further from the truth. You've climbed your peak, and now you're standing on the summit. What do you see?

More peaks! Higher than North Carolina's Mount Mitchell! All of them are waiting to be climbed.

Each represents challenges and rewards different from the one you just scaled. As Seneca said, "Every new beginning comes from some other beginning's end."

THE VALUE OF A GOOD CRY

MAY 24

Weeping is a positive part of being human.

The loss of a loved one, the agony of defeat, severe disappointments, and many other circumstances bring sorrow to all of us. The key to emotional health is to learn how to handle grief.

People who react to sorrow only with anger become embittered, hardened, and cynical. But people who show emotion through crying show they are not robots.

They feel. They react. They're moved, and their whole body quakes. Through it all, they learn how to deal with one of the toughest emotions in life.

Thus, they grow.

In the words of William Shakespeare, "To weep is to make less the depth of grief."

Or better yet, in the words of Theodor Geisel, better known as Dr. Seuss: "Don't cry because it's over. Smile because it happened."

SO MANY REASONS...

MAY 25

He was eighty-nine years old, a dentist in Duluth, Minnesota, and he had more patients than ever in his life.

His hands were steady, his peers considered him competent, and whenever anyone asked him about the possibility of retirement, he'd say with a twinkle in his eye, "I'll quit when they carry me up the hill. Feet first!"

Now, meet a man in his early twenties. On many Friday nights, he meets his friends at a local restaurant, and whenever the subject comes up about work—about anything—he always has a standard reply: "I always try to find a good reason to get out of bed."

With everything within us—heart and passion, perseverance and purpose—we were **not** created to do anything that we **cannot** do.

And age has little to do with it.

The world is full of good reasons for getting out of bed. Pulling teeth may not be your thing, but your mind and body are full of potential.

Identify it. Develop it. Use it.

CREATE A NEW VISION

MAY 26

When you think you've reached the point at which you can stop all forward progress and stand pat for the duration, you're in danger.

Look around you for another exciting challenge. Form a new vision, and commit once more to its fulfillment.

When you do that, you will create for yourself a future of never-ending challenges, achievements and excitement.

You must be better tomorrow than you are today, just to stay even.

DON'T LET CRITICISM FLOOR YOU

MAY 27

When you ask for feedback, you have to be willing to accept negative criticism. Don't let it clobber your self-esteem. Unless you know what's **wrong**, you can't fix it.

But don't take all criticism at face value.

Criticism springs from different motives. Some people may hold back negative criticism for fear of offending you and losing your friendship. Others may look only for the negatives, believing that by minimizing someone else's achievements, they can make themselves look wiser or more successful.

Dr. Norman Vincent Peale's advice to me years ago was profound: "Listen to criticism from others. If it is merited, heed it. If not, ignore it."

YOUR FIRST STEP

MAY 28

The road to success begins with the question: What do you want to do?

You've heard that question often.

You come home Friday evening and your spouse asks, "What do you want to do this weekend?"

And you shrug.

"I don't know," you respond. "What do **you** want to do?"

And since neither of you is willing to make a decision, you end up doing nothing in particular. Before you know it, it's Monday again and all you've accomplished is getting the Sunday paper read.

Many people let their early adulthood slip away in just this way. They waste too much time, and before they know it, they have families, mortgages, orthodontist's bills, and college tuition to pay, and they never answer the question, "What do you want to do?"

The earlier you confront that question, the better. At any age, you can decide what you want to do with the rest of your life. It's never too late.

GET A SET OF WINGS

MAY 29

S uccess in almost any undertaking requires that you engage in risk taking and with each risk comes the element of fear.

How you respond to the fear makes the difference between success and failure.

If you cower before it, running for cover at the first hint of disaster, you will fail. If you meet it boldly, letting it motivate you to action, you will succeed.

Think of our country's history. Our country was built on risk. The process of growing and learning always involves risk. Everything from the smallest entrepreneurial business to our country's space program was built on it.

As science-fiction writer Ray Bradbury said, "You've got to jump off the cliff all the time and build your wings on the way down."

Spread your wings today.

THE GRANITE WALL

MAY 30

I t sits thirty minutes south of Greensboro, North Carolina, in a grassy bowl beside a rest stop where the trees, bushes, and huge brick facade deaden the roar of interstate traffic. Standing there, surrounded by thirty-six crape myrtles, is one long, granite wall that contains names of someone's brother or sister, father or son, close friend or college buddy. It's the North Carolina Vietnam Veterans Memorial, with 1,598 names of native sons and daughters lost in a war four decades ago.

Go there today, and every name you see—on a brick, plaque, or yellow ribbon—tells a story. Calvin Cunningham has one.

When he goes there, he looks for the name Jacob H. Cunningham III, his older brother who called him "Calvo." Jacob was killed on Valentine's Day in 1967, when Jacob was twenty and Calvin was seventeen.

Calvin is now an attorney and grandfather, and he helped to create the wall in 1991. When asked why he did it, he talks about that fateful day—the knock at the door, the two soldiers he met, and the seventeen-word telegram about his brother's death.

"It's a life-altering event, and you know, it never leaves you," Calvin Cunningham says. "Never. It's always there."

Something to think about today on Memorial Day.

The need to remember. The need to see and stop a veteran. The need to say thanks.

A SUREFIRE FORMULA FOR CHANGE

MAY 31

Change is challenging, stressful, and often uncomfortable. To deal with it successfully, you need to be healthy in body and mind. Physical fitness, therefore, is an important asset for anyone coping with change. It gives you both physical and emotional energy.

To have a healthy mind, you need other people. Good communication with peers is a source of emotional strength for dealing with change. You'll feel better when you're able to talk over your challenges and opportunities with people who understand them and who sympathize with you.

Set aside time to think about the changes you anticipate. If you understand the causes and probable effects of the changes, you'll be in a better position to deal with them.

Keep your perspective. Take a balanced approach. Confront the challenges, but find time to enjoy yourself too.

And cultivate a sense of humor. Humor is the pleasant lubricant of life. If you approach change with a sense of humor, you'll take the sharp edges off the adjustments and smooth the way for you and those around you. As poet Marianne Moore put it, "Humor saves a few steps, it saves years."

You can't deal with change by resisting it. You have to accommodate it.

JUNE

THE PERSPECTIVE OF THE PALE BLUE DOT

JUNE 1

Like a snow-topped rock monster coming from the ground, the Andes Mountains look impassable. But from a jetliner flying at forty thousand feet, they shrink to manageable size. From the space shuttle, they're hardly noticeable at all.

The difference is in perspective—and that is so important to have.

People often fail to look at their lives in perspective; they are so concerned with immediate things, they don't bother to take the long view. That's because they don't expect to go very far.

When we see things in perspective, we see them in their proper relationships to their value and importance. And there is no better example of that than thinking of where you stand right now.

Here's how astronomer Carl Sagan describes it:

There is perhaps no better demonstration of the folly of human conceits than this distant image of our tiny world. To me, it underscores our responsibility to deal more kindly with one another, and to preserve and cherish the pale blue dot, the only home we've ever known.

Acquiring perspective enables you to respond realistically to the events in your life. Take this example of a teenage student with a broken heart.

His girlfriend just dumped him, and he is convinced that romance has died forever. His mom, though, looks at it from the perspective of years. She knows that the next "true love" is just a wink, and a smile, away.

DON'T RELY ON THE GRAND SLAM
JUNE 2

D on't rely on the grand slam. And don't swing for the fences.

Ask any baseball manager, and they'll tell you that it isn't often a player hitting a home run with the bases loaded wins the game.

Games are usually won by scoring one or two runs at a time. Those who pin their hopes on the one big swing are waiting for a moment of glory they're likely to experience only in their imaginations.

Don't wait for that perfect pitch to arrive in the perfect moment. Take advantage of every moment available, and remember this:

- ❂ The important sale is the one you are attempting to make now.
- ❂ The big break you are looking for is the opportunity that presents itself now.
- ❂ Your best bet for a good job is to do the best you can with the one you have right now.

IN SEARCH OF HAPPINESS

JUNE 3

Putting activities ahead of values may involve you in an endless rat race that leads to few lasting rewards.

If you settle upon activities rather than values as your core motivation, you greatly narrow the scope of your efforts and greatly restrict your prospects for happiness.

People who put career first may end up with gold-plated résumés and rusted-out family lives. People who put sports, music, and entertainment first may go through life having a ball, but go home in tears after the ball is over.

Happiness isn't the same thing as having a ball. Happiness comes when you search for meaning, purpose, and strong personal relationships. When you find those things, happiness will come.

Take heed of the words from the Dalai Lama: "Happiness is not something ready made."

ATTITUDE IS EVERYTHING

JUNE 4

In the early twentieth century, a complicated process called "linking" was needed to produce embroidered stockings. It was difficult to train people in the skills of linking, and nine out of ten newcomers who tried to learn quit before they mastered the process.

The critical steps were executed in the mind, not in the hands. Skilled workers could tell you the mechanical steps involved, but they couldn't describe the mental processes that guided these steps.

They had acquired them unconsciously as they worked and weren't even aware of what they were.

Of course, the time-and-motion expert the factory hired couldn't observe them. So the factory hired a trainer named Pearl King.

King didn't watch. She did the work. It took her twenty-six days to learn to perform the task slowly but accurately.

She discovered the subtle clues that could not be picked up by observing. Then she developed a formal training program to teach the skills to others.

We learn some things through observation and formal instruction. For other tasks, there's no substitute for getting your hands dirty…and **doing**.

Confucius said, "I hear and I forget. I see and I remember. I do and I understand."

Pearl King understood that.

JUST DO IT

JUNE 5

People with bad attitudes do not usually feel very good about themselves—or anyone else. Even when they're having a good time, they're not happy. They think to themselves, *This won't last.* They can come up with too many reasons not to be happy.

With a good attitude, you don't dwell on the bad aspects of your life. You allow yourself to enjoy the good times. With a bad attitude, you waste good moments worrying about the past or dreading the future.

Christian evangelist Leonard Ravenhill once said this: "The opportunity of a lifetime must be seized within the lifetime of the opportunity."

Carpe diem. Seize the day.

BRILLIANCE IS NOT SUCCESS

JUNE 6

You don't have to be brilliant to be successful. People with seemingly ordinary gifts have made extraordinary contributions to society. The secret lies in determining where your strengths lie, then focusing those strengths on your objectives.

It works.

Ron Wanek was the only son of a poor sharecropper in Minnesota. He went no further than high school. But he worked his way up in the furniture business. That became his university. He got to know people, to understand marketing strategies and manufacturing methods, and turned Ashley Furniture into the world's largest furniture retailer.

Some call Wanek the Steve Jobs of the furniture industry, and he comes to High Point University often to share his experiences with students.

So, it can happen. Simply be relentless. You'll get better every day.

WHAT DOES SUCCESS MEAN TO YOU?

JUNE 7

N o one else can define success for you.

Luciano Pavarotti's mother wanted him to become a banker. But that wasn't Pavarotti's definition of success. He wrote his own definition and became what he wanted to be—a great operatic tenor.

For Donald Trump, success meant making lots of money. For Ted Turner, it meant building the CNN media empire, one that could challenge the major networks. For Mother Teresa, it meant ministering to the needs of the destitute in India.

What will it take to make **you** feel successful?

That's a question you have to answer for yourself.

TWO SIMPLE WORDS

JUNE 8

Legend tells us that the sages of ancient Greece—the philosophers, statesmen, and lawgivers who laid the foundation for western culture—gathered in Delphi and inscribed "Know Thyself" at the entry to its sacred oracle.

Subsequently, those two words became the touchstone of western philosophies and stretched far beyond this town in Greece.

Since then, those two words have been passed down through the ages, and they still hold true today for all of us.

As you constantly attempt to stay true to the deep values that have become a part of your life and act in a manner consistent with those values, you can find peace of mind, happiness, and success in life.

All with the help of those two words. Know thyself.

Still good advice.

YOU'RE BETTER THAN YOU THINK

JUNE 9

Most of us tend to react more sharply to pain than we do to pleasure. We tend to feel our losses, failures, and difficulties more intensely than we do our wins, gains, and joys.

Here's a way to keep your perspective: Keep score of your victories. Write them down, keep a list where you can review it often, and collect mementos of your victories, including pictures, online recognition, and awards.

You might be surprised at how many of these things you can legitimately gather. When you do, you'll realize that you're probably better at what you do than you think.

It's your life. Celebrate it.

A LESSON FROM DENZEL

JUNE 10

We all know the Oscar-winning actor Denzel Washington from his movies. And **yet**, there is another side that doesn't come through on the big screen.

Washington is the son of an ordained minister and reads his Bible every day. He is married with four children and says his "ultimate dream project" is his children.

He sees acting as a way to make a living. But his family? That is his life.

"My faith helps me understand that circumstances don't dictate my happiness, my inner peace," he said.

You too can find that peace of mind. Remember your values. Like Denzel Washington, it'll help you define your path.

THE COLOR OF FAILURE

JUNE 11

In the early stages of the Industrial Revolution, a four-sided piece of wood meant everything to a worker. It was about two inches long and one inch wide, hung over each workstation, and painted a different color on each side.

Each day, the superintendent would turn the side to the color he thought denoted the employee's performance for the previous day—black for bad, blue for so-so, yellow for good, and white for excellent.

You can imagine the effect this had on morale. People who consistently got blacks and blues were constantly worried about their jobs, and this worry was just another drag on their performance.

In the short term, fear may have driven the so-so performers to perk up for a while. But in the long term, fear is a poor incentive.

In the old days, the black side of the block was, in effect, a public reprimand. Even today, reprimanding before others is a sure way of murdering morale. Public praise and constructive criticism in private is the formula for building morale.

If you let people know that you expect excellence—and reward them when they achieve it—you get long-term results. The reward may be nothing more than a public acknowledgment of their achievement.

But it boosts morale. Guaranteed. So who needs a block?

WHAT TO ASK YOURSELF

JUNE 12

When we invest our lives in responding to urgencies, we allow circumstances and other people to choose for us how we will live.

The only cure for wasting our lives putting out brushfires is to have a specific and clearly focused objective that we should be working on at any given moment.

When we know what objective will move us closer to our goals, then we can weigh the urgency of a circumstance against what is really important to us.

What is really important to you?

DON'T MISS YOUR CHANCE

JUNE 13

Jesus taught that those who do well with what they are given will be given more. Success comes to truly successful people as a series of little successes rather than one big break. Nobody's going to hand success or happiness to you on a silver platter. Success seldom comes quickly, and it almost never comes easily.

Most of us miss our best opportunities in life because they come disguised as hard work.

Start looking for opportunities today. You never know.

OUR BEAUTIFUL CONSTELLATION

JUNE 14

B etsy Ross could work a pair of scissors. She could cut a five-pointed star with a single snip. When a friend from church came to her house one day in May 1776 to ask if she could sew the first flag, she said yes.

Her church friend was George Washington. Ross was handy with a needle and thread, and had even embroidered ruffles for Washington's shirt and cuffs. And she needed the business.

She was a widow struggling to run her own upholstery business, which included making flags. That's what Washington, along with wealthy landowner Robert Morris and Colonel George Ross, the uncle of her late husband, came to ask her about.

On June 14, 1777, the Continental Congress adopted her handiwork as our national flag under the Flag Act—"Thirteen stripes, alternate red and white; that the union be thirteen stars, white on a blue field representing a new constellation."

At High Point University, we proudly fly the American flag because it represents in red, white, and blue the opportunities given to all of us. It helps us remember the spirit that created this country. And for many, it's not just pretty words.

According to President Woodrow Wilson, "The flag of the United States…has been created by the experience of great people, and nothing is written upon it that has not been written by their life. It is the embodiment, not of a sentiment, but of a history."

VIVID IMAGES WE NEED

JUNE 15

Like a fine camera capturing the essence of a moment, vivid, memorable images capture the essence of a message.

Canadian physician John McCrae immortalized the fallen American soldiers sleeping in a Belgian graveyard with this simple, vivid, and memorable imagery:

> *In Flanders fields the poppies blow.*
> *Between the crosses, row on row*

Recall, too, the memorable words of astronaut Neil Armstrong as he stepped from his lunar module and planted the first human footprints on the moon: "That's one small step for a man, one giant leap for mankind."

And think of the vivid image NBA star Kevin Durant left in our minds when he was named the league's MVP in 2014—and thanked his mom:

> You kept us off the street, put clothes on our backs, food on the table.
> When you didn't eat, you made sure we ate. You went to sleep hungry.
> You sacrificed for us. You the real MVP.

These images are easily visualized and capture the spirit of the message. They leave mental pictures in the minds of the listeners that will help them remember the message.

You can do that too.

YOUR TRUE MVP

JUNE 16

Nobody on earth is more valuable than you are.

Your life is as precious to you as the greatest people's lives have been to them. And your estimate of your self-worth is the only estimate that counts. What other people think about you is your **reputation**. What you think about yourself represents your **true worth**.

Thomas Edison's teachers thought he was just another hard-of-hearing, slow-witted kid. Edison knew better, and he showed them.

You are a bundle of potential. All you need to do is to convince yourself that the potential is there—and develop it.

THREE PHASES TO THINK ABOUT

JUNE 17

P roblems, left unaddressed, will move through three stages:

- ✪ **The proactive stage,** when they can be solved fairly simply.
- ✪ **The reactive stage,** when remedial steps are necessary to turn the situation around.
- ✪ **The crisis stage,** when immediate action is required to avoid permanent damage.

Some people seem to live constantly in the crisis phase. Others seem to go through life avoiding the rough times. How do they do it?

By addressing problems while they're still in the proactive stage. This prevents unimportant things from turning into urgent situations that divert your time and attention away from important things.

MOSES, THE DELEGATOR

JUNE 18

When the Israelites were wandering in the wilderness, Moses tried to shoulder the burdens of everyone. Day in and day out, he would sit and listen while people brought him their problems.

Then his father-in-law, Jethro, made a suggestion. Instead of making all the decisions yourself, why not delegate? On Jethro's advice, Moses appointed subordinates who oversaw groups of Israelites.

He gave them the laws and principles to go by, but left it to them to make the decisions. When a problem couldn't be solved within a smaller group, it was passed up to the higher level. Only the most difficult problems or the ones involving the entire nation were brought to Moses.

You can benefit from Jethro's advice. We all can.

You don't have to shoulder the problems of everyone in the organization.

You don't have to make a decision every time a subordinate comes to you with a problem.

Delegate responsibility and accountability. Empower those below you on the organizational chart. You'll be surprised at the wisdom they display, and at the burden they'll lift from your shoulders.

And you'll create a sense of teamwork in a successful community.

THE POWER OF SMALL THINGS

JUNE 19

Historian Will Durant often talked about how he had looked for happiness in knowledge, in his travels, and in his writing only to be constantly disillusioned, filled with worry, and fatigued.

In his book, *Steps to the Top*, Zig Ziglar shared a story about how Will Durant caught a glimpse of the true nature of happiness.

He saw a woman in a tiny car with a child sleeping soundly in her arms. Then, a man came along.

He sat down in the car, leaned over, and kissed the woman, softly kissed the child, and the two adults smiled at each other. And then the family drove off. Durant later observed something that should stick with all of us: "Every normal function of nature holds some delight."

Fill your life with those small moments that burst with delight.

WATCH FOR WHALES
JUNE 20

A submarine finds its way through the dark ocean deep by sending out sound waves or sonar. These waves bounce off objects and rebound toward the submarine.

But sending the signal is only half the job. If nobody is there to hear the echoes, the submarine navigates blindly. If the sonar operator doesn't know what to listen for, the navigator may mistake a whale for another submarine—or worse yet, another submarine for a whale.

If you don't learn to listen, you might as well be a submarine heading toward a whale.

Conversation is a two-way process. By listening skillfully, you can judge whether the other person understood. And vice versa.

Heed some advice from David King, the chairman of Laboratory Corporation of America in Burlington, North Carolina:

One of the things that made me different, particularly as an employer, was that I tried to listen. A very smart person said to me when my mouth is open my ears are closed.

HANG IN THERE

JUNE 21

If what you are doing is worth doing, hang in there until it is done. Some won't understand. But that's okay. There will always be critics and skeptics who are unwilling to try something themselves but will ridicule and criticize the person who plods on despite the circumstance.

Look at Abraham Lincoln. He was called "a gorilla" and "a buffoon" and labeled by one of his peers "an embarrassment to the republic."

I'd tell you who those critics were, but here's what's funny. Nobody seems to remember their names.

So hang in there. Your future is bright.

THE NEED TO BELIEVE

JUNE 22

Consider:

- After Fred Astaire's first screen test, the memo from the testing director of MGM, dated 1933, said, "Can't sing. Can't act. Can dance a little." Astaire kept that memo over the fireplace in his Beverly Hills home.
- Socrates was called "an immoral corruptor of youth."
- Drew Brees was called "too small and too much of a risk" for any NFL team after his shoulder surgery in 2006.

Successful people know that there will always be three kinds of acquaintances: those who want you to succeed, those who want you to fail, and those who don't care.

They use the first group as sources of encouragement. They use the second group as incentives to prove the doubters wrong. They ignore the third group.

Brees ended up leading the News Orleans Saints to the Super Bowl—and winning—while helping to inspire a city devastated by Hurricane Katrina.

We all know Astaire could dance. As for Socrates, he went on to be one of the founders of Western philosophy.

Not too bad.

FOCUS ON THE FUTURE

JUNE 23

Successful people learn to pass up immediate pleasures in return for more gratifying long-term pleasures. They do the dull and unglamorous things that unsuccessful people are unwilling to do.

By doing so, they avoid the recurring crises that result from neglecting things of long-term importance.

Take Father Horace McKenna, for example. He worked tirelessly throughout his life for the rights of the poor in Washington, DC, helping to develop a low-income housing community, founding a soup kitchen, a clinic, a jobs center called SOME (So Others Might Eat), as well as Martha's Table, which serves the needs of homeless women.

He died in 1982 at the age of eighty-three.

Martin O'Malley, the former governor of Maryland, met Father McKenna as a teenager. Here's how he described McKenna's focus on creating a better future:

He gave his entire life to serving the poor, and he truly did see the face of God in every individual he served.

EXPLORE THE POSSIBILITIES

JUNE 24

The trouble with many plans is that they are based on the way things are now. To be successful, your personal plan must focus on what you want, not what you have.

If you focus on what you have, your future will be limited by your present circumstances.

If you focus on what you want, your imagination will be set free to explore the possibilities.

YOUR CREATIVE POWERS

JUNE 25

The human mind—coupled with an indomitable spirit and a marvelous, physical body—is capable of creating in a way unknown anywhere else in the universe. Even when the physical body is limited, the human mind and spirit can break free to create in the most amazing ways.

Consider Christy Brown. He was an Irishman born with cerebral palsy. He could only control his left foot, but that didn't stop him. Brown became a painter, writer, and poet.

He wrote his autobiography in 1954 and his life was made into a movie in 1989. The talented actor Daniel Day-Lewis portrayed Brown.

The movie's title? Appropriately, *My Left Foot*.

Here's how Brown describes the freedom painting brought him:

Painting became everything to me. Through it, I made articulate all that I saw and felt, all that went on inside the mind that was housed within my useless body like a prisoner in a cell.

Think like Christy Brown. If you would reach your full potential, cultivate all of the creative urges within **you**, and respond to the sensitivity that cries out for expression…

Imagine what could happen.

LOOK INWARD FOR EXCELLENCE

JUNE 26

The quest for excellence is an inward one. You won't find it in a book or seminar or in an expensive piece of high-tech equipment.

You'll find it within yourself.

There is a quote often attributed to popular author J. R. R. Tolkien. Whether he wrote it or not, it speaks volumes. The quote goes like this: "It is not the strength of the body that counts, but the strength of the spirit."

Look inward so you can find your own source of excellence.

MONEY ISN'T THE ROOT OF ALL EVIL

JUNE 27

You've often heard people say, "Money is the root of all evil," claiming they're quoting from the Bible.

Well, the Bible doesn't say that.

What it does say is that the love of money is the root of all kinds of evil. The love of money is what often induces people to kill, rob, or commit other crimes.

A balanced view of money is **nothing** like that. It takes into consideration its value in your life: what you will do to get it and what you will do with it after you get it.

LEAVE THE PAST IN THE PAST

JUNE 28

If you want to move ahead, you can't focus on the past or even the present. The only place left to build your life is in the future.

Take Ezra Klein, for example. He worked as a blogger and columnist at *The Washington Post* and became hugely successful. But he bet his own brand was better than the *Post*'s legacy brand, and he struck out on his own, launching the independent news site Vox.com.

Klein didn't let the future happen. He created it. You can too. You create it by forming a clear, vivid picture of what you want and fixing your mental and emotional eyes on that picture.

Let it become your vision, and it will draw you toward its fulfillment.

TO BE MARCUS

JUNE 29

M any people deny themselves the pleasure of living life to the fullest because they follow limited visions. They dream modest dreams, so they compile modest achievements. The limiting factor is not their capacity to achieve but their willingness to believe in themselves.

Don't let self-doubt stand between you and what you desire. You can achieve what you want to achieve, provided you believe in yourself and depend on God.

Roman Emperor Marcus Aurelius put it this way, freely translated: "Do not think that what is hard for you to master is humanly impossible. And if it is humanly possible, consider it within your reach."

THE GOOD BOOK SAYS...

JUNE 30

I choose to see myself, and all other humans, as the creative expression of a loving God. The book of Genesis says that God, the sovereign of the universe, breathed into our nostrils and gave us life. He created us in His own image.

In other words, each of us carries a part of the divine. Only when we are committed to excellence can we begin to measure up to all that we were created to be.

At High Point University, we say this: "Choose to be extraordinary."

We know God wants it that way.

JULY

THREE CATEGORIES OF ACQUAINTANCES

JULY 1

Always think about the **right** 25 percent.

Twenty-five percent of the people you know will always wish you success. Another 25 percent will always hope you fail. The rest are trying to make up their minds.

People who worry about what other people think are likely to be indecisive. They are preoccupied with the 50 percent who are making up their minds because they worry that this group will join the 25 percent who long to see them fail.

And what happens? People who worry about the 50 percent worry a lot. Successful people don't do that. They zero in on the 25 percent of people who they know wish them well, and they use comments from that corner like a basketball team relies on cheers from their home crowd.

Successful people know they'll always be there.

They also rely on the 25 percent who don't wish them well, using insights from that crowd in the same way a basketball coach writes a disparaging remark or a previous losing score across a locker room's blackboard to motivate the team.

Successful people aren't concerned about the other 50 percent. They see no need to waste energy on a group of people who won't change.

So why should you?

WINNERS AND LOSERS

JULY 2

There is a difference between winners and losers.

Losers respond to circumstances; winners create circumstances.

For example, if you live way up north, you can stay inside during the winter and complain about the snow and the cold. Or you can take up skiing and sledding.

If you live in a big city, you can complain about traffic congestion and the cost of parking. Or you can carpool or take the bus.

If you're a high school graduate, you can complain about the lack of jobs for people without a college degree or technical training. Or you can go out and get an education.

Create your own circumstances. A computer science professor did. He once said, "We all have finite time and energy. Any time we spend whining is unlikely to help us achieve our goals. And it won't make us happier."

Randy Pausch said that in September 2007 after he was told he had no more than six months to live. His lecture turned into a book, *The Last Lecture*, which turned into a bestseller.

Pausch was named as one of the world's "100 Most Influential People" by *Time* magazine. A big *Star Trek* fan, he also got a bit role, saying four words in film director J. J. Abrams's reboot of *Star Trek*.

Pausch died at age forty-seven in July 2008. He showed all of us that if you don't like the way things are, complaining won't change them. Action will. He took action and so can you.

TO BOLDLY GO...

JULY 3

W e must all hang together, or assuredly we shall all hang separately."

Benjamin Franklin said that to his fellow patriots at the signing of the Declaration of Independence.

The delegates who signed their names to the document were opening themselves to the charge of treason, a capital crime.

We all know what happened. Against great odds, the colonies won their independence.

The men who signed the Declaration didn't stick their necks into a noose blindly. They were deeply committed to their cause and believed the consequences of inaction were as great as the consequences of failure.

They had an army under a capable general and had the advantage of defending familiar terrain against an enemy from far away with a long and tenuous supply line.

Still, they were a wilderness nation up against a world power, and their faith in their cause—and their knowledge of the consequences of defeat—led them to take the bold risks that led to eventual victory.

You can beat the odds too. But always be sure that the potential gain is worth the risk and that you stand a realistic chance of succeeding.

OUR "AMERICAN MIND"

JULY 4

America. Land of the free. Home of the brave. Remember that today, on our Fourth of July.

It's a great opportunity to renew our dedication to the principles of liberty and equality enshrined in what Thomas Jefferson called "the declaratory charter of our rights and the rights of man."

As a practical matter, the Declaration of Independence publicly announced to the world the unanimous decision of the American colonies to declare themselves free and independent states, absolved from any allegiance to England. But its greater meaning was a bold statement that we—our country—would be ruled by the people, for the people.

It expressed, in the words of Jefferson, the "American mind."

The great historian Samuel Eliot Morison stated its importance eloquently: "If the American Revolution produced nothing but the Declaration of Independence, it would have been worthwhile."

Today, keep joy in your life even when it seems difficult to do so.

We cannot forsake our tradition and forget our legacy. We can only pray, hope, work, and persevere.

We are all created for a purpose—one grander and better than we could ever imagine. Our lives aren't measured by success, but by significance and our commitment to our faith, dedication to our family, and loyalty to our friends.

Celebrate that today.

ETHNICITY CAN FOOL YOU

JULY 5

An American of European descent sat down at a banquet table next to a man who he thought was Chinese, and in an effort to be friendly, the American turned to him during the soup course and asked in a halting, easy-to-understand voice, "Like soup?"

The American didn't get a response.

When the principal speaker was introduced, the American was surprised to see the man he thought was Chinese walk to the podium and give a brilliant address in a fluent, Midwestern accent.

As he sat down, he turned to the American and asked, "Like speech?"

Ouch.

Remember: the skin color, ethnic background, or accent of an individual tells you nothing about the individual's abilities.

Learn to appreciate the differences among people and celebrate the similarities.

LEARN TO FLY

JULY 6

P atrick Overton wrote this poem back in 1975 as part of his book *The Leaning Tree*. So many years later, its five lines still ring true.

> *When you come to the edge of all the light you have*
> *And take that first step into the darkness of the unknown,*
> *you must believe that one of two things will happen:*
>
> *There will be something solid for to stand upon,*
> *or, you will be taught how to fly.*

"You will be taught to fly." A great line to remember on any day.
So on this day, fly like an eagle and find your own infinite skies of potential.

THE POWER OF YOU

JULY 7

We often worry about so many things we can't control.

Like what others do to us and what happens to us. Or where we are born and what physical impairments we have. Or how much money we start out with and what others expect of us or how high our IQ is.

Instead, think about what you can control—how you react to what others do to you, how you cope with what happens to you, how well you use the physical abilities you have, how you respond to the opinions of others, and whether you can—or will—live up to others' expectations.

It's what you do with your IQ, not how high it is.

As the late, great poet Maya Angelou once said, "You may not control all the events that happen to you, but you can decide not to be reduced by them."

Remember that today.

FIRM FOOTING

JULY 8

William Faulkner once gave some very good advice to a student: "I have found that the greatest help in meeting any problem...is to know where you yourself stand. That is, to have in words what you believe and are acting from."

David King, CEO of Laboratory Corporation of America has a take on the same thing. At High Point University, he told students: "You must have a point of view. Leadership is all about having a point of view."

THE IMPORTANCE OF SMALL SUCCESSES

JULY 9

Getting organized is simply a means of survival. If you spend most of your day trying to get things together so you can get started on your goals, you are setting yourself up for frustration.

Who needs it?

One of the greatest reasons people cannot mobilize themselves is that they try to do great things. Most worthwhile achievements are a result of many little things done in a single direction.

CHALLENGE YOURSELF

JULY 10

S uccess is like a muscle. You must work it.

Think about it this way. You must exercise your muscles or they won't grow. You have to do more repetitions or lift more weight, and you must be consistent about it, or you won't see any changes in your body. Discipline is the key.

A workout with a feather pillow won't do.

The same goes for success. You can pursue easy goals all year long, and they won't stretch you. Your performance won't get better because you're not challenging yourself to get better.

At first, it may be a matter of guessing about what is beyond your grasp and what is too easily gained. But with a little experience at setting and reaching goals, you will learn what goals are appropriate for you.

The key? Start now.

VALUE PEOPLE; USE THINGS

JULY 11

P eople who are happy and successful learn to value people and use things.

Those who are looking for something to make them happy somehow never seem to find it. Yet those who find a way to be happy while they are looking benefit in two ways.

Not only are they usually happy while they are looking, but also they typically find what they are looking for.

As philanthropist John Ruskin said more than a century ago: "He only is advancing in life whose heart is getting softer, whose blood warmer, whose brain quicker, and whose spirit is entering into living peace."

BE LIKE HANNIBAL

JULY 12

You can't dream your way into the future. You need a plan.

You have to know where you want to go and decide how you're going to get there. The important word here is **how**. The word **if** won't take you there.

To achieve your vision, you must approach it with a positive attitude, a sense of certainty that your dream is achievable. You must adopt the attitude of Hannibal, the great general from ancient Carthage, who said, "We will either find a way, or make one."

A plan will establish a route to your destination and provide for the elimination of roadblocks. It will also blaze new trails across uncharted territory and prevent you from drifting aimlessly through life.

Who wants to do that?

WALK THE WALK

JULY 13

I t is a mark of insecurity—not of self-confidence—to always be talking about your abilities and accomplishments. Holding your abilities and deeds in perspective is not only important in maintaining friendships, but also goes a long way toward building self-confidence. Here are some notable descriptions of how holding your tongue…helps:

- ❂ Novelist William S. Burroughs said, "Jesus Christ said, 'By their fruits ye shall know them,' not by their disclaimers."
- ❂ Sir Francis Bacon described it this way, "The less people speak of their greatness, the more we think of it."
- ❂ George Akomas Jr., an entrepreneur and motivational speaker, was a bit more succinct when he said, "Walk the walk… Talk ain't necessary."

ARE YOU A SWAMP OR A RIVER?

JULY 14

A swamp goes nowhere. Its soggy soil will bog down those who try to make their way through it, and it breeds mosquitoes, snakes, and maybe even alligators. Moreover, its waters stagnate and produce foul odors. Swamps are best left to the creatures who inhabit them.

Now, a river is a dynamic thing. It provides a habitat for a variety of fish. It serves as an artery for pleasure and commerce. Its rushing waters can provide energy for industry and home. If obstacles are thrust in its path, it goes around them or over them. If necessary, it will cut a new channel.

Some people are like swamps. They go nowhere and often slow down those who do try to make progress.

Others are like rivers: constantly on the move, brimming with energy, ready to deal with whatever obstacles stand between them and their goals.

Which one are you?

FINDING YOUR PERSONAL HARMONY

JULY 15

What are sound principles?

They are based on your rock-bottom assessment of what is right and represent your perception of the way things ought to be in relation to your values.

If you want to be truly happy, direct your efforts toward bringing your life into harmony with the way things ought to be.

All the talent in the world will not bring you happiness if it is not applied in harmony with this perception of the way things should be. Applying your talents without reference to your values and principles is like using your car's accelerator without touching the steering wheel.

It may take you far and fast, but it probably won't take you where you want to go.

Most of us see life like a split image viewed through the lens of a camera. One image represents reality: the way things are. The other represents our principles: the way thing ought to be.

Successful people bring their lives into focus by merging the two images.

When we perceive the way things are as the way things ought to be, our lives are in harmony.

WHAT REALLY COUNTS

JULY 16

People with a winner's attitude know that fame and fortune are not the only measures of success and that public recognition and money are only superficial ways of keeping score.

What drives the winners to put forth a Herculean effort—to bounce back from failures and defeats, overcome handicaps, and battle discouragement and fear—is the knowledge that they are involved in a purpose that is bigger than they are.

Life is about **influence** and **impact**.

Influence others in healthy ways. Impact the world with your work and your life.

CREATE A NEW SCRIPT

JULY 17

To guide your future, you have to make an irrevocable commitment to act. You do this by wiping the slate clean, creating a new script, and embarking on a course from which there is no turning back.

What's past is past; what's done is done.

The important thing is what you can do **now** to achieve the future you want. This requires a willingness not only to accept change, but also to pursue it **proactively**.

Look ahead with faithful courage.

THROUGH THE EYES OF A CHILD

JULY 18

People who asked the type of questions children ask and then looked for answers have made the great discoveries of the universe.

Take Albert Einstein. He gained insight into the nature of gravity when he questioned why we don't feel gravity while we're falling.

His theories of relativity rested upon such childlike questions as "Does the train pull away from the station, or does the station pull away from the train?"

But you needn't be an Einstein to open the doors to creativity. Just look at the world through the eyes of a child, ask those childlike questions, and let your intuition provide the answers.

Try that today. What will you discover?

THE SELF-CONFIDENT FOCUS MODEL

JULY 19

People who have strong self-confidence tend to apply their personal power to useful goals. They let others talk about their abilities and deeds. They concentrate on goals, not activities. And they freely express admiration and appreciation to others.

It is enough for them to know the value of their goals and to believe in their abilities to reach those goals. They are far more concerned that their actions speak louder than their words.

They are walking examples of that verse from the New Testament, 1 John 3:18: "Dear children, let us not love with words or speech but with actions and in truth."

FROM WALDEN POND TO WALL STREET

JULY 20

Many highly creative people have a casual indifference toward their personal appearance, but in reality they are making a purposeful statement. They are saying, in effect, "I'm so good at what I do that I don't have to dress for success."

Henry David Thoreau was such a person. He wrote: "Beware of all enterprises that require new clothes."

If you plan to spend your life in the seclusion of a place like Walden Pond, follow Thoreau's advice. But if you want to make it on Wall Street—or Main Street in your hometown or beyond for that matter—pay careful attention to the clothes you wear and the visual impact you have on others.

An artist may dress like an artist. Entertainers can be creative and daring in their attire. People who work with tools and machines should dress with an eye for practicality. People who spend their time interacting with other people in the business world should dress to the standards of those with whom they deal.

After all, a first impression is a lasting impression.

THE BOLL WEEVIL: A HERO?

JULY 21

In Enterprise, a small town in southeastern Alabama, the town's trademark is a large statue of a boll weevil.

Why would any town honor a destructive pest like the boll weevil?

Here's why: Many years ago, the entire economy of Enterprise was based on raising cotton. It was simply a poor, little farming community with no future. Then, several years in a row, the boll weevil wiped out the entire cotton crop for miles around. The people were starving.

Someone stepped forward and suggested that the town diversify its crops and try to attract some industries. That's exactly what happened.

The result? A thriving, broad-based economy.

Had it not been for the boll weevil, they might be still tied to cotton.

Sometimes a problem that causes major difficulty may be the prod that triggers a vault to success.

THE PEASANT, THE KING, AND THE GOLD

JULY 22

Once, a peasant offered to pay the king an extra farthing in taxes if the king would let him see the royal treasury, where the gold was kept. The king, ever alert for a chance to augment his fortune, let the peasant have a look.

The peasant peered at the heap of shiny yellow metal and remarked, "Now I'm as rich as you are."

The king was puzzled.

"This room holds more than half the gold in the kingdom," the king said, "and it all belongs to me. How can you be as rich as I?"

The peasant replied: "You have all this gold and all you do is look at it. Now, I have looked at it too."

Covet not. Savor the chance to enjoy life.

BE LIKE MIKE AND HAMMERIN' HANK

JULY 23

Two athletes. Different eras. Same drive to win.

Henry "Hank" Aaron, a member of the Baseball Hall of Fame, hit 755 home runs during his twenty-two-year career. He once said that if he came to bat in the ninth inning and his team had an eight-run lead, he'd go for the home run. If he came to bat with the bases empty, two out, and his team in desperate need of a score, he would also aim for the fences.

But with the crucial run in scoring position and one man out, he would go for percentages. He knew he was far more likely to score the runner with a single rather than with a big swing that could end in a strikeout or a pop fly.

Michael Jordan, the basketball superstar, scored thirty-nine points in game two of the 1992 NBA Finals. But his Chicago Bulls lost in overtime to the Portland Trail Blazers, 115–104. The next game, he began feeding the ball to his teammates. Jordan scored twenty-six points. But the Bulls won and ended up winning the series 4–2.

The principle applies in life as well. When people compete with one another for glory in an organization, only the competition wins.

When they cooperate internally, they become more competitive externally—and the entire organization wins.

ONE BOOK AT A TIME

JULY 24

If you stack thirty-six books one on top of the other, it looks like a hopeless stack of reading. But if you aim to read three books a month, you'll finish all thirty-six in a year. And you'll probably do more reading than the person whose target is "to read everything I can get my hands on."

It's that way with goals. The future you desire may seem impossibly far away. But if you move toward it one goal at a time, you will achieve it faster than you thought possible.

ANALYZE THE RISKS

JULY 25

The process of risk analysis is not that complicated. Before embarking on an undertaking, examine the venture and answer these questions:

- What is the best thing that could happen as a result of this action?
- What is the worst that could happen as a result of this action?
- What is the most likely result of this action?

If the **most likely** result would take you toward your vision, and you're willing to deal with the **worst possible** result in exchange for a shot at the **best possible** result, go ahead with the venture.

THE MERCY OF THE DICE ROLL

JULY 26

The choice between what's important and what's unimportant in your life can be made either consciously or unconsciously.

The husband and father who spends most of his time in front of a TV ignores the activities of his household and neglects the training of his children. To him, TV is important.

The woman who spends her bonus on an expensive new sports car instead of investing it in a retirement fund decided that present pleasures are more important to her than future comfort.

A few people have followed unconscious choices to spectacular success because their choices happened to place them in the right places at the right times. Others have meandered through life pursuing whatever passion dominated at the moment and ended up going nowhere.

Remember, unconscious choices put you at the mercy of the dice roll.

SELF–RELIANCE BREEDS SELF–ESTEEM

JULY 27

The people with the healthiest self-esteem are those who have learned to stand on their own two feet.

They are willing to pass up the fun-for-the-moment experiences and select a course that pays off in the long run.

Of course, all of us yearn to be free. But your best chance of remaining free is through self-reliance. Here is an adage to remember: "He who pays the piper, calls the tunes."

Only when we are self-reliant can we maintain our self-respect and keep our widest options.

THE TRUMAN SHOW

JULY 28

When Harry Truman became president upon the death of Franklin Roosevelt, many considered him to be the most unprepared person ever to assume the office.

And he took over in the most critical of times. During the first days of his presidency, he told a group of reporters: "Boys, if you ever pray, pray for me now... I've got the most terribly responsible job a man ever had."

This ex-farmer, unsuccessful haberdasher, and small-time Missouri politician hadn't even gone to college.

And yet, he had to negotiate with the likes of Winston Churchill and Joseph Stalin and the question of nuclear weapons, the existence of which had been unknown to him before taking office. In addition, he had to help rebuild Europe, stop communism overseas, and turn Japan into a friendly democracy.

At home, Truman dealt with aggressive labor leaders, defiant segregationists who resisted his efforts at dismantling racial barriers, and virulent red-baiters who were willing to sacrifice democratic principles in their zeal to exterminate communism.

Were all of Truman's decisions the correct ones? Of course not.

But his standing as a leader is unquestioned. Truman refused to underestimate himself. He believed in himself. He once said: "America was not built on fear. America was built on courage, on imagination and an unbeatable determination to do the job at hand."

CLEAR THE AIR
JULY 29

There's a story about what happened when evangelist Billy Graham flew into Dallas to address the student body of a large seminary. A storm had moved in and visibility at the airport became so low that his plane couldn't land. It had to circle over the city for several hours, long beyond the time of his scheduled appearance.

But no one on the ground knew that his plane couldn't land. Afterward, he told an audience what he learned from his time in the air and fog:

> It occurred to me while I was up there circling around that as preachers, we spend most of our time circling around in a fog, while people are wondering where in the world we are.

It's a condition that plagues people in any business, any relationship, or any family. The high art of plain talk is simply saying something so that it can be understood. And it's the best way to clear away the fog from all your attempts to communicate with anyone.

FOCUS ON THE IMPORTANT

JULY 30

A major difference between an amateur and a professional in any calling is a pro's ability to focus on important tasks by minimizing urgent tasks.

You minimize urgent tasks by spotting problems while they're still minor and easily remedied, and taking care of them at once.

Say you spot a loose shingle on the roof; you replace it to prevent the leak that could threaten to ruin your antique armoire.

Say a customer calls you with a minor service problem; you take care of it right away to prevent you from losing a major account.

It all boils down to this: if you keep in perspective what's really important, you won't spend all your time doing what seems urgent.

IN SEARCH OF INNOVATION

JULY 31

C reativity may be the agent of change, but innovation is the agent of excellence. The difference is subtle—but significant.

You see it in the business world. Innovation establishes a defining line between managers and leaders. Managers deal with the present reality and try to make it work under new circumstances. Leaders improve on the present reality to meet the future's requirements.

Look at it this way: learning puts you in touch with the past, but innovation puts you in touch with the future. And you too can cultivate the quality of innovation by thinking outside conventional channels. Here's how:

- ✪ **Never become married to an idea.** Walk away from ideas that don't work and go looking for something that will. You can learn from failures and build upon this knowledge.
- ✪ **Prowl for new knowledge.** Always be reading a new book, exploring new places, absorbing new experiences, and drawing on the knowledge and experiences of the people you meet.
- ✪ **Don't be afraid of the future.** See it as an adventure, not as a looming storm. The status quo is expendable. There is no such thing as the "new normal." In your world, you must remember: change is constant.

AUGUST

THE ONE QUESTION TO ASK YOURSELF
AUGUST 1

What do you enjoy doing?

Ask yourself that question and it'll help you identify three things: your **congenial competency**, the activity that allows you to use your best talents in an enjoyable and satisfying way; your **compatible career**, a line of work that allows you to use your congenial competencies in a profitable way; and your **congenial role**, a position within a compatible career that lets you follow your normal behavior pattern most of the time.

Biz Stone found all three. He liked to design software, and when his friend, Evan Williams, formed a communication start-up that pushed podcasting, he realized something basic: you have to be emotionally invested in what you do.

And he wasn't emotionally invested in podcasting. He didn't like it. But he knew what he did like. He liked expressing himself by letting other people express themselves. That philosophy fit into how he saw his professional world: people first, technology second.

Then one day, while tearing up the carpet in his house, he got a text message from Williams: Sipping pinot noir after a massage in Napa Valley.

Stone belly laughed because he couldn't believe the stark difference between what he and his friend were doing. And in that moment, he knew what he wanted to build.

Twitter.

DESTINY OR DETERMINATION?

AUGUST 2

The old peasant just didn't know.

A wizard had asked him what he wanted to be. Well, the peasant was a stable hand, a laborer, and he struggled to give the wizard any kind of answer.

"Make up your mind," the wizard told the peasant. "Then, when I come back by in a couple of weeks, I'll grant your wish."

So the peasant started noticing those around him.

He saw the miller. His job was too strenuous. He saw the cobbler. His job was too time-consuming. He saw his boss, the nobleman. His job had too many responsibilities.

Then he saw a baby. The old peasant knew. "I want to be a baby," he told the wizard. The wizard granted his wish.

Fifty years later, the immortal wizard came to that very same stable and saw the very same peasant cleaning out the stable.

That saddened the wizard. He realized the old peasant did become a baby. But when he grew up, he left his life to chance rather than deciding what he wanted to become and what he really wanted to be.

As you think about your future, remember the stable hand.

Control what you want to become.

SHOULD YOU?

AUGUST 3

The fact that you **can** do something doesn't mean that you **should** do it.

If you were going from New York to San Francisco, you **could** go by way of Miami. But it would be a roundabout way and a waste of time unless there was something important you needed to do in Miami.

Your car might be able to travel at 110 mph, and you could floor it. But it would be foolish and dangerous to do it on the freeway en route to work.

Or it might be possible for you to buy a new Mercedes sports coupe. But if your goal is to own a condo in Aspen, the Mercedes purchase might push the condo into the distant future.

It's important that you identify your goals and spend your time—as well as your energy and resources—on things that will lead you toward your goals.

LIFE IS A GRINDSTONE

AUGUST 4

S omeone said that tears wash the soul.

American theologian Harry Emerson Fosdick put it this way: "Life asks not merely what can you do; it asks how much can you endure and not be spoiled."

Josh Billings, the American humorist, had another take: "Life is a grindstone, and whether it grinds a man down or polishes him up depends on the stuff he's made of."

Be open to possibilities.

IF YOU FINISH SECOND, YOU LOSE

AUGUST 5

Richard Petty began his spectacular stock-car racing career by finishing second. Excited over this achievement, he rushed home to his mother. "Mama! There were thirty-five cars that started, and I came in second in the race!"

"You lost!" his mother replied.

"But, Mama!" he protested. "Don't you think it's pretty good to come in second in my first race—especially with so many starters?"

"Richard," she said sternly, "you don't have to run second to anybody!"

For the next two decades, Richard Petty dominated stock-car racing. He never forgot his mother's challenge.

Winners compare their achievements with their goals and with their own potential. The rest compare themselves with others.

STOKE YOUR FURNACE

AUGUST 6

Life is too short for you to settle for second best in your career, in your personal life, or in any of your significant relationships.

Any goal that does not take into account all three areas is not worthy of your pursuit.

Whatever keeps you from reaching your goal for today had better be important because it's costing you a day of your life.

Goals aren't complicated. They are simply a way of breaking a vision into smaller, workable units to get you where you want to go.

"Goals," said bestselling author Brian Tracy, "are the fuel in the furnace of achievement."

KEEP MOVING
AUGUST 7

Words from American naturalist and nature essayist John Burroughs: "There is a condition or circumstance that has a greater bearing upon the happiness of life than any other… It is to keep moving."

He compares our lives to a stream of water. His conclusion: "If it stops, it stagnates."

Make inertia work for you.

DON'T STOP THE TIDE

AUGUST 8

The Danish king, Canute, heard that his courtiers believed he could stop the tide from coming in simply by issuing a command.

He didn't believe that, and to teach his followers a lesson in the limitations of power, he had his throne carried to the seashore. As the tide came in, his courtiers quickly learned that Canute—no matter how wise or how just—was not omnipotent.

"Let all men know how empty and worthless is the power of kings," said this modest ruler, "for there is none worthy of the name, but He whom heaven, earth, and sea obey."

Canute knew that he could neither stop the tide nor arrest the progress of history. He did not try to preserve the status quo. Instead of accepting the historic enmity between England and his Viking people, he became a peaceful ruler of both, promoting trade and arts.

Some people believe that they can reverse the tide of change and return to some idyllic past—and prosper—just standing firm.

But change is just as inevitable as the tide. Don't try to stop it. Accommodate it, channel it, and use it. But don't try to stop it.

FAR FROM DEAF

AUGUST 9

Thomas Edison learned the telegrapher's trade while working for the Michigan Central Railroad.

At first, the signals were transmitted in the form of dots and dashes scratched on a piece of paper. Later, the signals were transmitted in the form of audible clicks. Edison was hearing impaired and couldn't hear the clicks.

He didn't waste time trying to improve his hearing, and he didn't strain his ears trying to hear the clicks. Instead, he invented a telegraph that could convert the electric impulses into letters of the alphabet.

Sometimes people waste their time trying to do the impossible, or they throw up their hands and surrender to their circumstances.

Successful people do what Thomas Edison did: they create new circumstances.

THE OIL OF EVERYTHING

AUGUST 10

Some people can get extreme. You know a few of them.

They interrupt people at will, and they say what's on their minds without regard for other people's feelings. They think the world should run on their schedule, and they show up for appointments when it's convenient. If they keep others waiting, that's tough.

To them, concessions are for weaklings and diplomacy is useful only as a manipulative tool.

Such people may be able to bulldoze their way to success for a while. But when they encounter reverses of fortune—and they find themselves in need of supporters—they'll run into a rude awakening.

They'll find more gloaters than sympathizers. Courtesy is the oil that lubricates the machinery of commerce, and it can smooth the path to success in sales, in management, in personal relationships, and in life.

It's like the old proverb, "To speak kindly does not hurt the tongue."

It won't. So be courteous to someone today.

See what happens.

PRACTICE MAKES SUPERB
AUGUST 11

A young musician listened with awe as a piano virtuoso poured all his love and skill into a complex selection of great compositions.

"It must be great to have all the practicing behind you and be able to sit down and play like that," he said.

"Oh, I still practice eight hours every day," the master musician said.

"But why?" asked the astounded young man. "You're already so good!"

The old man shook his head. "And I want to become superb," he responded.

School is never out for the pro. In a world of 7.1 billion people, where their competition comes from every corner of the globe, make the investment to become superb.

Pros can't afford not to be.

WHERE IS THAT HORSE?

AUGUST 12

S uccessful people are optimistic. If you expect failure, that's what you'll get. If you expect to succeed, you're far more likely to achieve success.

Many people go through life looking for things to criticize or complain about. Others can find something positive in nearly every development.

They're like the little boy President Ronald Reagan liked to tell about. When he got a large pile of manure for Christmas, he began digging into it.

"With all this manure," the boy said, "there's got to be a pony somewhere in here."

A positive attitude won't remove all the challenges from your life. But it will be of tremendous help in overcoming them.

TEN RULES YOU NEED

AUGUST 13

H ere are ten simple rules that will help you minimize the stress in your life. Follow them. Think about them. See what happens and reward yourself when you follow them.

1. **Relax over breakfast.** Start your day right.
2. **Organize your work.** Create your to-do list early and do one item at a time.
3. **Allow yourself to be imperfect.** It's okay. We all are.
4. **Don't do it all.** The best word to remember? No.
5. **Don't take your work home with you.** Home is a refuge, not a workstation.
6. **Shut out unnecessary noise.** Recognize the therapeutic nature of silence.
7. **Let people know what bothers you.** Usually, they don't mean it. Tell them.
8. **Take a break.** Don't eat at your desk. Take a walk. Read. Recharge.
9. **Develop stress-reduction strategies.** It could be as simple a breathing deeply.
10. **Learn to laugh.** Laugh at yourself. Life is too short.

LIFE IN THE BRIAR PATCH

AUGUST 14

In Joel Chandler Harris's tales of Uncle Remus, the hero is a brash rabbit who constantly outsmarts the fox. On one occasion, the fox catches the rabbit and tries to dream up the most dreadful means of doing him in.

"Don't throw me in the briar patch," the rabbit pleads. The fox does just that.

The briar patch, of course, was the rabbit's home. He knew all the secret entrances, all the hidden trails. He loved the challenge of hopping through the thorny passageways—and outwitting his enemies.

Many people feel that way about their niches in life. They find their jobs stimulating, their companions congenial, and their lifestyles satisfactory. They can find all the challenge they need right there in the briar patch.

If you're in a comfortable briar patch, you don't have to leave it for greener fields just because somebody tells you things are better beyond the hedgerow. But you do need to stay prepared for changes.

Keep abreast of developments in your field and in other fields that interest you. Briar patches don't last forever. Often, they get cleared away for new developments.

If that happens, you'll want to be prepared.

THE NUANCES OF HELPFUL PEOPLE

AUGUST 15

P eople with a positive self-image tend to be genuinely helpful to others.

In fact, the two tendencies go together so well that it is hard to tell which produces the other. It is probably a little bit of both. Those who feel good about themselves long to help others feel good about themselves. The more they reach out to help others, the better they feel about themselves.

Only the insecure, the frightened, or those with low self-esteem approach life with an attitude that says, "It's every person for himself or herself."

Sadly, they find only more insecurity and lower self-esteem.

TIME NEEDS TO BE YOUR FRIEND

AUGUST 16

Peter Drucker, known as the father of American management, has some advice for you:

Time is the scarcest resource and unless it is managed, nothing else can be managed.

To manage your time, manage your habits. Our brains are programmed like giant computers to enable us to do routine things without thinking about them. If we don't consciously program routine activities, they program themselves. But how do you do that?

- ✿ **Clarify your objectives.** Think about the steps you need to take to reach a goal and estimate how much time it'll take to do that.
- ✿ **Analyze your time habits.** Keep a time log and see how long activities take to see what robs your time.
- ✿ **Keep a to-do list.** Do that for daily and weekly tasks to free your mind from nagging worries and define what is important.
- ✿ **Get yourself organized.** Don't shuffle papers. Act on them immediately. Prioritize tasks and keep it simple.
- ✿ **Cultivate a time management habit.** Delegate responsibilities.
- ✿ **Control telephone usage.** Keep time in meetings to a minimum.
- ✿ **Take time for your goals.** That includes fun.

It's your life. You need to live it.

"LET ME DO IT NOW"

AUGUST 17

He was known citywide as a miserly grouch, and as he lay on his deathbed, surrounded by his family, he called for his lawyer.

The lawyer came with the man's will in hand. The man asked him to read it. The last line caught everyone by surprise. It read: "I leave all my fortune and worldly goods to charity, and none to my family, because I want a lot of people to be sad when I die."

What a terrible way to ensure that everyone will miss you when you're gone.

There is a better way to make the world know you have been here. It is to leave the lives of all you touch enriched. Stephen Grellet did.

He was a Quaker missionary who was born in France, and he died in New Jersey in 1855. You may have never heard his name, but certainly you remember these familiar words:

I shall pass through this world but once. Any good therefore that I can do or any kindness that I can show to any human being, let me do it now. Let me not defer or neglect it, for I shall not pass this way again.

Those words resonated with Henri-Frédéric Amiel, a Swiss philosopher who said, "He who is silent is forgotten;…he who does not advance, falls back; he who stops is overwhelmed, distanced, crushed; he who ceases to grow greater becomes smaller; he who leaves off, gives up; the stationary condition is the beginning of the end."

Never stand still. Good advice.

PLANT YOUR OWN APPLE TREE

AUGUST 18

Many people go through life feeling isolated, never comprehending what it means to reach out and touch someone.

You've probably seen them. You probably know quite a few and hear them tell you, all flush faced, in a rush of words: "It's a dog-eat-dog world out there! You've gotta look out for yourself!"

But wait a minute. Think about what is around you. You need to accept the wonderful reality that you are part of the human race. You, me, and everyone around us are brothers and sisters of humankind. Pick up the rhythm of your humanity and remember the thought of poet Carl Sandburg: "A baby is God's opinion that the world should go on."

It's hard to think like that when the world around us has become so divisive, where terrorists kill people in the name of religion and people distrust others because of the color of their skin or the place where they worship.

But don't give up hope. Remember these words from theologian Martin Luther: "Even if I knew that tomorrow the world would go to pieces, I would still plant my apple tree."

He said those words more than five hundred years ago. They are still true today.

SOMETIMES YOU MUST EXPLAIN VERY CAREFULLY

AUGUST 19

There was a time during World War II when you could travel to the most remote parts of America and people didn't know about Winston Churchill, Pearl Harbor, or Franklin Roosevelt. That didn't help when anyone went there to sell war bonds to raise money for America's military.

Consider this story about the importance of communication. A bonds salesman stopped by to see a farmer out and asked, "Wouldn't you like to help out by buying some war bonds?"

"Reckon not," replied the farmer.

"Wouldn't you like to join the defense effort with Mr. Roosevelt?"

"Nope, reckon not."

"Aren't you upset over what they did to Pearl Harbor?

"Reckon not."

"Don't you want to be on the side of Churchill?"

"Nope."

"So you don't want any bonds?"

"Nope."

Frustrated, the salesperson moved on.

The farmer's wife came over and asked about the stranger in the barnyard.

"Some fellow had a story about a guy named Roosevelt who got a woman named Pearl Harbor in trouble over on the side of Church Hill and wanted me to go to his bond."

Sometimes, you have to explain very carefully.

WRITE YOUR PERSONAL MISSION STATEMENT

AUGUST 20

S it down and ask yourself these three questions: What am I passionate about? What are my values? What makes me great?

This will help you write your own personal mission statement. We all need one. It will help crystalize what things inspire and energize you while providing you a path toward success and giving you permission to say **no** to things that are distractions.

To write one, here are some instructions: Make it brief and simple, and write it in present tense. Then go public with it. Tell your friends and family what you expect to achieve.

Afterward, frame it and put it in a place where you can see it every day. Your friends and family will see it too. If you do that, the vision of yourself gains power—and it gives you an extra incentive to achieve.

Here is an example of one mission statement: "To be a teacher. And to be known for inspiring my students to be more than they thought they could be."

A television executive wrote that with her grandmother in mind. She remembers watching her grandmother wash clothes in a cast-iron pot and hang them on the line. The executive knew she wanted to do more with her life than hang clothes on the line. She wanted to become a teacher.

But she became more than that. Her name is Oprah Winfrey.

THE NORTH STAR OF YOUR LIFE

AUGUST 21

S tart by planning backward in time to the present. It begins with your vision. Your vision represents your overall objective in life. You won't achieve it in a day, probably not in a year, and perhaps not in a decade. But you want to make steady, measurable progress toward your vision.

You can do that by setting definite goals: long-range, medium-range, short-range, and immediate.

Long-range goals are broad objectives that will require sometimes as much as a decade or more to achieve. Medium-range goals are more specific. They take one to five years to achieve and specify the things you need to accomplish to achieve long-range goals.

Short-term goals usually encompass time periods of less than a year. They tell you what you should be doing in the near future to accomplish the medium-range goals. Immediate goals are things you should be working toward right now to take you toward your short-term goals.

To pull this off, get your laptop or a pad and set daily, weekly, and monthly goals to carry you toward your broader goals. The shorter the time period involved, the more specific your goals should be.

Put a date beside each one and make a commitment to reach that goal by that date. Make them reasonable. But set goals that will stretch you. Review them daily.

What you wrote will become the North Star of your life.

BE THE HOMELY HEN

AUGUST 22

Through goal setting, you can:

⚙ Direct your time, energy, talents, and skills into areas where they will be most effective in taking you toward your vision.

⚙ Make the most effective use of your congenial competencies—the activity that allows you to use your best talents in an enjoyable and satisfying way—by using them to establish a pattern of success.

⚙ Identify the results you expect to achieve, measure your progress toward these results, and make mid-course corrections where necessary to assure that you achieve results.

⚙ Identify the obstacles in the pathway of success and deal with them.

Then, when you reach them, celebrate to boost your morale and acquire the emotional energy to your next goal. And tell people. Why? Consider this anonymous poem:

> *The codfish lays ten thousand eggs,*
> *The homely hen lays one.*
> *The codfish never cackles*
> *To tell you what she's done.*
> *And so we scorn the codfish*
> *While the humble hen we prize,*
> *Which only goes to show you*
> *That it pays to advertise.*

REMEMBER YOUR "GOOD HOURS"

AUGUST 23

Memories **don't** just happen. You have to make them happen. But how? Here are some tips:

- ❋ **Practice awareness.** Too many people sleepwalk right through their most beautiful moments in their lives.
- ❋ **Receive love from others.** Share the precious moments of your life with others you care about. Make a special effort to include them in as many memory-building moments as possible.
- ❋ **Don't let worries push out your awareness.** Yesterday's problems, failures, and missed opportunities, along with the anxiety of tomorrow, can elbow out **today's** joys.
- ❋ **Stay in touch with your inner self.** We all need time at various stages of a busy day to get in touch with God, with ourselves, and with the deep, underlying purpose for which we work and live. We need some "me time" to reflect.

If you do these, you'll cement good memories in your mind. It helps to remember these words from poet Ralph Waldo Emerson: "To live the greatest number of good hours is wisdom."

WISDOM: YOUR ULTIMATE ASSET

AUGUST 24

Wisdom is information sharpened into a tool.

We begin with a body of information, then hone it and improve it. In time, the information develops into a reservoir of knowledge and, at some point, becomes wisdom. When we apply information and knowledge with wisdom, our words and actions influence others. We become persons of substance.

Information is the foundation of wisdom. We can't act wisely without accurate information. Therefore, to influence others constructively, we must acquire knowledge.

But learning that knowledge leads to wisdom can't be obtained haphazardly. It must be purposely **sought**, and the search for knowledge must be constant. By applying this knowledge to everyday challenges, we build up a body of experience, and that experience leads to wisdom.

If all you have is information, people will use you and then discard you. If all you have is knowledge, people will need you until such time as their own level of knowledge is equal to **yours**, or is, in their view, sufficient.

But if you have wisdom, people will respect you.

So, every night, ask yourself this question: What did I learn today that I did not know yesterday?

THE IMPORTANCE OF LEGACY

AUGUST 25

Fame and fortune are fleeting because time can dim the memory of who we were and what we did. Fortunes can evaporate, and even if they don't, we can't take them to the grave.

But a legacy is different. It is what you bequeath to humanity. If it's a good legacy, its benefits will remain long after your name has been forgotten. Your family will rejoice in it. And you'll have invested your energy in helping to build a better world.

What your legacy is depends on what you choose to put at the center of your life. You can make riches and fame your twin goals. Or you can choose to make this planet a better place for the humans on it.

Before he was thirty, Albert Schweitzer had won worldwide fame as a writer and theologian, as an organist and an authority on organ building, and as an authority on Johann Sebastian Bach. But he is remembered today for founding a hospital in the remote backwoods of Gabon in West Africa.

That was his legacy. Of his work, Schweitzer once said, "Seek always to do some good, somewhere. Every man has to seek in his own way to realize his true worth. You must give some time to your fellow man. For remember, you don't live in a world all your own. Your brothers are here too."

A thought to be taken to heart.

TO CATCH YOUR TOUCHDOWN PASS

AUGUST 26

You must act today. You know, as in carpe diem. Seize the day. But here's the thing: you must keep focused on your tomorrows.

If your vision does not extend beyond today, then you will become mired in failure because success in life **can't** be achieved in a single day.

Take Bill Walsh. He's a retired NFL coach, winner of three Super Bowls, and a member of the Football Hall of Fame. Here is his take:

> Perhaps the secret to effective action lies in how you interpret the length of the "day" in carpe diem. If it's a moment or a day, you're cutting down on the odds for success. But if you recognize that in business as in sports (or all of life, for that matter) there's a season made up of several opportunities, those odds go up considerably.

But opportunities are like touchdown passes. You have to catch them to win. Walsh adds:

> The key to success is reaching out, extending yourself, striking, and then, if you fail, bouncing back and doing it again—being so resourceful that finally when the moment comes again you won't hesitate.

Hesitation results from uncertainty about where you want to go and what you want to do to get there. To seize your day, you must have a purpose.

That, you must know.

YOUR NEW TOOL

AUGUST 27

Make it a habit to go about every day looking for things that you can change for the better. It may be something as simple as a minor change of routine. It could be a new hairstyle, a new approach to your wardrobe, or a new route to work.

Here is one rule of thumb to follow: when you've done something the same way for at least two years, there is probably a better way of doing it.

Playwright George Bernard Shaw lived in an age when the pace of change was slower. But he was always examining new ideas. Here's what he said:

It is an instinct with me personally to attack every idea which has been full grown for ten years.

Take that as good advice. If you don't learn to move with change, you'll soon find the world moving ahead while you lag behind.

In the past five years, think about the three major changes in your life and ask yourself these questions: Did you initiate the change? If not, did you anticipate it? Did you resist these changes or welcome them? What future changes do you anticipate and how do you expect to deal with them?

If you have drifted into these changes, you need to acquire the tools of CHANGE: that is C for Creativity, H for Healthy Habits, A for Accommodation, N for Nose for News, G for Good-bye to the past, and E for Eagerness to Succeed.

CHANGE. A good tool to have.

EDUCATION IS THE KEY

AUGUST 28

An anonymous sage once ventured to say this about education: "Education is what you have left over after you have forgotten everything you've learned."

That's a powerful insight. With education, learning becomes a renewable resource.

Training is imitative; education is creative. The difference between a trained person and an educated person is the difference between a parrot and an orator.

Training teaches you to solve problems according to procedures others have tested and proved. Once you've learned the procedure, you keep repeating it for as long as the task is useful. When the task is no longer useful, the skill is no longer valuable.

Education teaches you to develop your own procedures, solve your own problems, and move on to other challenges. It can enable you to put old skills to new uses or to develop new skills for new challenges.

So remember this today: Training is a program that has a beginning and an end. Education is a process that has a beginning and no end.

YOUR PATH TO A GOOD MEMORY

AUGUST 29

There is this electrical engineer named Matt.

He can remember telephone numbers of colleagues, friends, and family members from long ago, and it always amazes his coworkers. So, one day, one of them asked how he did it.

Matt had an answer.

"Most of us have conditioned ourselves to say, 'I have a terrible memory!'" he said. "But it's simple really. You have to control the mind and make it do what you want it to do."

How, right? Here are some tips:

- **Desire is the key to remembering.** Take time to realize the value of what you are trying to remember and reinforce it by reminding yourself that this memory can enrich your life.

- **Write it down.** It helps in two ways. First, anything you visualize is always easier to remember. Second, it's like the Chinese proverb:
  "The palest ink is better than the best memory."

- **Read your notes out loud.** As you say the words, it will pull the item to be remembered up from your subconscious and reinforce your memory.

- **Review your notes.** Go over what you write until it is firmly fixed in your mind.

- **Promise yourself.** Really, promise yourself and you'll remember.

THE BIGGEST MISTAKE

AUGUST 30

The only way you can avoid making mistakes is to make the biggest mistake of all—do nothing. Some mistakes truly hold serious consequences—sometimes far out of proportion to the ease with which they are made.

But no failure, misfortune, or mistake is ever so great that nothing good can come from it.

As David Starr Jordan, the founding president of Stanford University, said, "Wisdom is knowing what to do next, skill is knowing how to do it, and virtue is doing it."

LEAD WITH YOUR HEART

AUGUST 31

Suppose you want to learn to fly an airplane. Would you want to take lessons from someone who has never been in the cockpit?

Suppose your instructor was to tell you, "I've explained to you all you need to know about flying an airplane. Now I'm going to try it myself. I'm going up to practice what I preach."

Wouldn't you feel a lot safer if you knew he was preaching what he had already practiced?

If you're going to lead others, you must first acquire competence in the field in which you expect to lead. Then you can ask others to follow you.

The substance behind your preaching lies in your heart and your mind. It is the sum of what you've experienced, what you've learned, and who you are. If people are to listen to you and follow you, they must be convinced that there is genuineness at the core of your being.

Think of Nelson Mandela. He spent twenty-seven years as a political prisoner, and after his release from prison, he became the first black president of South Africa. After his release, he said:

> Our human compassion binds us the one to the other—not in pity or patronizingly, but as human beings who have learnt how to turn our common suffering into hope for the future.

SEPTEMBER

THE VISION OF COACH PARKER
SEPTEMBER 1

Corey Parker coaches football at a high school south of Detroit, where his players know poverty, violence, and broken homes firsthand.

All that hits close to home. Coach Parker's players remind him of his younger self. He grew up in a tough Detroit neighborhood. He got out when he received a scholarship to play college football, and he now talks about college with his players all the time. His coaching has worked.

In 2013, nine out of fourteen graduating seniors earned college football scholarships at a school where fewer than two-thirds of young men graduate on time.

Coach Parker sees football as the backbone in having his players believe in themselves. In 2014, he told National Public Radio:

It's a good, strong backbone to let you know you are good enough, you are strong enough, you are smart enough to do anything you want in this world. To have vision, to have foresight, to have dreams… That's what football is.

When you can, be a coach. Mentor a young person and give them guidance. When you do, you gain a sense of fulfillment that won't go away. Self-interest is a wonderful thing, but enlightened self-interest is ten times better. It's not about what we get; it's about what we give.

THE NEED TO KNOW

SEPTEMBER 2

W e all need culture.

Being **cultured** doesn't mean that you have to recognize all of Beethoven's symphonies after the first few bars or be able to tell at a split-second glance what century Botticelli finished a particular painting.

But it helps to know enough about the fine arts to hold your own in conversations involving contemporary culture.

If you like a certain kind of music, by all means enjoy it. But occasionally listen to other types of music. You may find that you can enjoy Beethoven as well as the Beatles, Rachmaninoff as well as the Avett Brothers.

As you expand your tastes, you will find yourself comfortable with a broader segment of society and increasing your universe of sales prospects. Your new knowledge will give you a great deal more self-confidence, which will help you make a more favorable impression on a wider variety of people.

Others look up to people of manners, culture, and good taste. But you will notice something else as well.

Once you have acquired cultural polish, knowing that the Avett Brothers sprang from Concord, North Carolina, and Botticelli from Florence, Italy, you will become a different person, one who is broader in knowledge. In doing so, your world will expand and become a richer, deeper place.

WATCH YOUR TONE OF VOICE
SEPTEMBER 3

P oet G. K. Chesterton once went into a fish market, and in a low, endearing voice, he said to the female clerk waiting on him, "You are a noun, a verb, and a preposition."

The woman blushed, apparently flattered that such a cultured individual had observed such qualities in her.

After buying the fish, Chesterton exclaimed in a higher voice, "You are an adjective, an adverb, and a conjunction!"

The woman slapped him with a flounder.

Taken literally, Chesterton's words were meaningless. To call someone an adjective—whatever that means—is certainly no more insulting than to call one a noun.

But the tone of voice conveyed a meaning that the woman understood instinctively, and her response was instinctive.

Take notice of your tone of voice. Often, **how** you say it is more important than **what** you say. You should use different voice qualities when you want to express warmth, when you want to express enthusiasm, and when you want to express authority.

Practice putting these qualities into your speech. It will help you build your effectiveness.

FIND YOUR OWN MARK

SEPTEMBER 4

There once was a navy jet pilot who was terrified at first at landing his aircraft on the deck of an aircraft carrier.

"Everything was in motion," he said. "The ship was tossing up and down, the waves were moving, the airplane was moving. Trying to get it all to move together seemed impossible."

Sometimes life seems like that, doesn't it?

An old pro gave the young pilot some advice that solved the problem. "There is a yellow marker in the center of the flight deck that always stays still," the old veteran told him. "I always line up the nose of the plane toward that mark, and fly straight toward it."

That's pretty good advice for coping with change—and with stress. Always have a goal to work toward, and keep your eyes fixed firmly on it.

WRITE IT DOWN

SEPTEMBER 5

F loyd Wickman, one of the nation's top sales trainers, started out as a mediocre real estate salesperson.

Then he wrote on a blank business card, "Floyd Wickman, Million Dollar Club Member."

Within a short time, Wickman had quadrupled his sales, and he made the Million Dollar Club. And that was years ago, when the average home in his area sold for under $50,000.

Later, Wickman decided to become a professional speaker and trainer. Again he wrote down his goal: to address an audience of 2,300 people within five years. He made it with two months and three hundred people to spare.

Wickman became a firm believer in setting goals, putting them in writing, and keeping them constantly in front of his eyes.

The practice led him to a succession of successes and a rich, fulfilling life.

How did it start? By simply writing it down and making it real. Your future success depends on your present beliefs.

MULES AND THOROUGHBREDS

SEPTEMBER 6

A mule," wrote novelist William Faulkner, is an animal that "will labor ten years willingly and patiently for you, for the privilege of kicking you once."

Ed Temple, the Tennessee State track coach who worked with some of America's top women track stars, had a saying , "A mule you drive, but with a race horse, you use finesse."

Faulkner and Temple were articulating the popular view of the mule as a stubborn, balky, and uncooperative animal. The mule is easy to underestimate.

You get on a horse, and he'll step into a hole. A mule? He'll go around it, and if he comes to a bridge with a hole in it, he won't even cross.

What many take for stubbornness in a mule is really enlightened self-interest. A mule won't go where he perceives a hazard; a horse will blunder into danger. A mule will pace itself so that it can labor all day; a horse will run all-out until it drops.

The mule is more plodding, more deliberate than a thoroughbred. The thoroughbred is more nervous, more sensitive than a mule.

A mule wouldn't do well in the Kentucky Derby. A thoroughbred would be a miserable failure pulling a wagon or plow. You use each in the role it's best suited for.

Some people are mules; some are thoroughbreds. Wise leaders learn the difference and use this knowledge to help the people they lead make the most of their abilities.

MOVE INTO THE FUTURE

SEPTEMBER 7

The future is a place you've never been before, and many people are a little nervous about entering it. They prefer the safe, familiar circumstances of the past. But if you are trying constantly to relive the familiar past, you'll never enjoy the rewarding future.

The way to keep from reliving the past is to take that irrevocable step. Cut yourself off from past circumstances so that your only choice is to move ahead.

"Until one is committed, there is hesitancy, the chance to draw back, always ineffectiveness."

Scottish mountaineer and writer William Hutchinson Murray said that in the last century. And that belief never becomes antiquated. You will find all kinds of ways to make the dream you created come true.

The only path open is the one ahead. It focuses your energy and resources and multiplies your chances of success.

SOMETHING CLICKED

SEPTEMBER 8

M any years ago, a young man went to a Western Union office to apply for a job as a telegrapher. In those days, messages were still transmitted in Morse code through audible clicks.

The young man had no experience in telegraphy, but he had studied it at home, and he knew the code.

His heart sank as he walked into the office and looked over the crowd of people filling out application forms.

But when he sat down with his own form, he heard a clicking noise in the background. He stopped filling out his form and listened. Then he dashed into the nearby office.

Moments later, a man emerged and told the other applicants they could go home. The job had just been filled.

What got him the job?

The clicking noise was the sound of a telegraph receiver. The young man listened and translated the clicks into words: "If you understand this message, come into the office. The job is yours."

WATCH FOR CAVES

SEPTEMBER 9

Many people are not willing to pay the price to be successful.

Maybe that's why so many withdraw into comfort zones. They long for a place to rest, a place to be safe, a place to be comforted and coddled.

But comfort zones are like caves. Their darkness makes it hard to see, their walls box us in, and the stagnant air inside grows stale and becomes hard to breathe.

So watch for caves—or what some would see as a comfort zone. They all have low ceilings, and they keep us from stretching to our full height.

MACARTHUR AND HIS MOM

SEPTEMBER 10

The night before Douglas MacArthur took his entrance exam for West Point, he was all nerves.

"Douglas," his mother, Pinky, said to him, "you'll win if you don't lose your nerve. You must believe in yourself, my son, or no one else will believe in you. Be self-confident and self-reliant, and even if you don't make it, you will know you have done your best."

When the scores were announced, Douglas MacArthur's name was number one on the list.

It was that same self-confidence that led him island by island across the Pacific until the Japanese were driven back to their homeland. And it was that self-confidence that led him to plan the amphibious landings at Inchon that turned the tide in the Korean War.

True self-confidence is the result of ample competence, which comes from knowledge, skill, and expertise.

DON'T BURN DOWN YOUR HOUSE

SEPTEMBER 11

L ove is the most positive force on earth, and each of us needs to cultivate it because we obtain spiritual strength by reaching out to others. But how can we cultivate love toward those whom we instinctively dislike or resent?

Fake it until you make it. If you practice the principle of love, you will soon find your feelings taking their cue from your actions. Some ideas from personal development blogger Sandra Pawula:

- See this as an opportunity for personal growth.
- Remember that anger and aggression only bring unhappiness.
- Examine the emotions triggered inside you to understand why you feel this way.
- Look for good qualities, for common ground.
- Look inside you to see you can change your beliefs that cause unhappiness. What you think about makes a difference.

However you deal with people you dislike, it will be difficult. But those emotions can be overcome because you control them, not the person you dislike.

Banish hatred. It's the most destructive force on earth—and it does the most damage to those who harbor it.

Protestant minister Harry Emerson Fosdick has an idea why: "Hating people is like burning down your own house to get rid of a rat."

MORE THAN A PAYCHECK

SEPTEMBER 12

In today's business world, a well-educated person is far more valuable than a well-trained person. Employees who are well-trained but not well-educated may perform their tasks with skill, but they aren't motivated to look beyond the specific task.

Educated employees become partners. They see themselves as part of the organization. They share its goals, buy into its vision, are challenged by its setbacks, and exult in its success.

In January 2013, researchers with the Pew Charitable Trust found that a four-year college degree helped protect young people from unemployment, low-skill jobs, and lesser wages.

Statistics from the U.S. Census Bureau bear that out. A high school graduate will earn $1.2 million in his or her lifetime. A college graduate will earn nearly double that.

But it's more than a paycheck. When you get educated, you can become your best self in every possible way.

ALL WE NEED IS...

SEPTEMBER 13

To succeed, you must be able to deal with all sorts of people, listening to their ideas and observing their values without compromising your own principles.

You must be secure enough in who you are to take criticism from friend and foe.

When someone you love disappoints you, you can't let the disappointment destroy you.

You must respect the values and opinions of others without allowing others to control your life.

Is this a part of you who are?

A DAILY MANTRA TO REMEMBER

SEPTEMBER 14

M otivational speaker Og Mandino believes we need to live each day by a set of principles that can help ground us and give us direction despite the troubles we face. His principles are all about seizing the present. Today:

- ❂ I begin a new life. I will fill my mind with good thoughts.
- ❂ I will greet this day with love in my heart. I will make love my greatest weapon.
- ❂ I will persist until I succeed. I was not born into this world for defeat. I was born to win.
- ❂ I am nature's greatest miracle. I will believe in myself.
- ❂ I will live this day as if it is my last.
- ❂ I will be master of my emotions.
- ❂ I will laugh at the world. I will stop taking others and myself too seriously.
- ❂ I will multiply my value a hundredfold.
- ❂ I will act now. I will not practice procrastination.
- ❂ I will pray. When I pray, my cries will only be cries for guidance.

Do that today. See what happens. And remember this: "Hope is greater than history."

American statesman Dwight Morrow said that at the height of the Great Depression. America recovered. You can too.

MAKE YOU A WINNER

SEPTEMBER 15

In a truly free society, leadership cannot be exercised without the consent of the led. True leaders must lead in such a way that people will **want** to follow them. They must, in essence, become heroes to those they lead.

Those who would be heroes to others must first be heroes to themselves; they must believe in themselves and trust in their own sense of direction.

Venus Williams does. For years, she was one of the top tennis players in the world. Even after she battled an autoimmune condition that caused joint paint and sapped her energy, she continued to play and became a hero to the next generation of champions. She said, "Some people say I have attitude—maybe I do, but I think you have to. You have to believe in yourself when no one else does—that makes you a winner right there."

Nobody and no institution can invest you with greatness. They can only recognize the greatness within you when you have found it and recognized it in yourself.

Look in the mirror today and know that your decisions and what you accomplish depend on you. So arm yourself with self-belief.

You've earned it.

THE REAL IDEA OF PRETTY

SEPTEMBER 16

A proud mother watched as her young daughter looked at herself in a mirror before departing for a special event. Like all young girls, she was worried about her appearance.

"Pretty is as pretty does," the mother told her, repeating the adage she had heard from her own parents.

The mother was trying to stress the values parents have been passing on to their daughters for centuries.

But that phrase only scratches the surface. Her beauty doesn't stem from what she **does**; what she does stems from the beauty that she **is**. Pretty **does** as pretty **is**.

From a young woman's desire to be her most attractive self, we derive an important principle of achievement: Achievement doesn't result from what you **do**; it results from what you **are**. It all comes from inside you.

In our international economy, your knowledge and skills may only be as relevant as the latest trending topic on Twitter. But your values can guide you through this ever-changing world because there is one thing we all need to remember.

The relevance of our values never expires.

FOREVER YOUNG

SEPTEMBER 17

Juan Ponce de León never found the Fountain of Youth.

He did discover Florida. But this insatiable thirst to get a sip of that magic water more than five hundred years ago pushed León to drive his men through the Florida heat only to discover bugs, alligators, snakes, sinkholes, and natives.

It didn't end well for Ponce de León. In 1521, on Florida's Gulf Coast, he was shot in the thigh with an arrowhead carved out of fish bone. His wound got worse and eventually killed him. All because of his quest for eternal life.

Ponce de León is a cautionary tale of zeal taken too far. The quest for eternal youth is timeless, but you too can capture that state of mind without blazing through the swamps of Florida—or any other place—for a sip of magic water.

Heed the advice of Samuel Ullman, an American poet and humanitarian:

Youth is not a time of life; it's a state of mind; it is not a matter of rosy cheeks, red lips, and supple knees; it is a matter of the will, a quality of the imagination, a vigor of the emotions; it is the freshness of the deep springs of life.

Whether sixty or sixteen, there is in every human being's heart the lure of wonder, the unfailing childlike appetite of what's next, and the joy of the game of living. In the center of your heart and my heart there is a wireless station; so long as it receives messages of beauty, hope, cheer, courage, and power from men and from the infinite, so long are you young.

GATHER YOUR HARVEST

SEPTEMBER 18

We all want spiritual balance in our lives. Here are some suggestions on how to find it:

- **Cultivate a sense of wonderment.** Look at the world around you and take in what you see, smell, and hear. As poet Walt Whitman said, "I believe a leaf of grass is no less than the journey—work of the stars."

- **Ask fundamental questions.** Look at the big picture. What would it be like to travel at the speed of light? Why don't we feel gravity when we fall? These questions will help expand your mind and your sense of what is real.

- **Value intangibles.** Stop and smell the roses. When you do, you'll find love, joy, peace, kindness, goodness, faithfulness, meekness, and self-control. Call it gathering the harvest of spiritual fruit.

- **Turn your imagination loose.** Do that, and it can free your mind from the constraints of what is possible, showing you how to make your dreams come true.

- **Accumulate good memories.** Russian author Feodor Dostoyevsky wrote, "If a man carries many such memories with him into life, he is safe to the end of his days, and if one has only one good memory left in one's heart, even that may sometime be the means of saving us."

FACE IT: YOU'RE WONDERFUL

SEPTEMBER 19

M ake note of your accomplishments.

When you do, you encourage yourself to continue to strive for your goals, and you strengthen your positive attitude.

So many times, we are quick to kick ourselves. We can be our toughest critics. But we never get around to patting ourselves on the back. You don't want to become boastful and self-centered, but it never hurts to accept kudos when you deserve them.

So accept the fact that you are wonderful, and get on with life! Have a great day.

JOE'S ADVICE

SEPTEMBER 20

He founded his company on a shoestring, built it into one of the world's ten largest construction firms, and spelled out how he did it in his book *Anatomy of an Entrepreneur*. Here are some of Joe Jacobs's techniques. They could work for you.

- ⚙ **Get your thinking straight.** All communication begins with thoughts. Before you communicate your thoughts to the outside world, take time to organize them.

- ⚙ **Say what you mean.** In face-to-face communication, you must get your point across accurately the first time or your communication is futile.

- ⚙ **Be real.** Each of us has a personality, a blending of traits, thought patterns, and mannerisms that can aid us in communicating clearly. Be natural, and let the real you come through.

- ⚙ **Get to the point.** Be concise and don't waste words. To quote Winston Churchill, one of the great masters of language, "Short words are best, and the old words, when short, are the best of all."

Communication is essential to success in our changing world. But the greatest need is for understanding, for building bridges between human beings so we can make this earth the best possible home for the human race.

WHAT YOU NEED TO DISCOVER
SEPTEMBER 21

R egardless of what field you're in, there has to be a professional raison d'être—a reason for being what you are. Discover it, and you've taken that first step toward success.

How do you discover the role that offers you the best opportunity to wield your talents successfully?

Here are some questions that will help you identify it:

⚙   What is the guiding or controlling idea in my life?

⚙   What is my strategy for implementing that idea?

⚙   What are my three greatest strengths, and what am I doing to capitalize on them?

⚙   What are my three greatest weaknesses, and what am I doing to compensate for them?

Answer these questions and you'll have a pretty clear picture of who you are and what your most valuable assets are. Find a role that capitalizes on your strengths and do whatever you can to compensate for your weaknesses.

THE MOST IMPORTANT SKILL YOU NEED

SEPTEMBER 22

If you want to succeed in today's global economy, the most important skills you can acquire are the skills in interacting with people.

Skills that are applicable only to a single job are vulnerable to advancing technology. If technology provides a new way to do the job, the skills become obsolete.

People skills, however, do not become obsolete. They will serve you well in a wide variety of organizations. The ability to work with others becomes paramount. You'll need to be able to interact with others, provide leadership within team settings, and communicate clearly and assertively.

These skills can provide you with the flexibility to move into many different roles that will benefit your community, your family, and you.

THE PERILS OF POLLYANNA

SEPTEMBER 23

I t was 1913 when American author Eleanor Porter wrote the novel *Pollyanna* about a girl who refused to see the negative side of anything and who believed that silver linings existed behind the darkest of clouds.

It was a charming, bestselling story more than century ago. But today, when it comes to leadership, **don't** be a Pollyanna.

Encourage the people you lead to bring you bad news, and make it clear that you will listen to them and deal with the situation. If you ignore bad news, you do so at your own peril.

Consider what Thomas J. Watson Jr., the late CEO of IBM, once did. An IBM executive once told Watson he had made a mistake that cost the company $15 million.

"I suppose you want my resignation," he said.

Watson told him to go back to work. "I've just invested $15 million in your education," he said.

The IBM executive let his people know that they could come to him with bad news without fearing dire consequences.

You can bet that his subordinates kept him informed.

THE NECESSITY OF COLLABORATION

SEPTEMBER 24

P icture this:

    A high school teacher is administering an exam, and each student is expected to come up with the right solutions to the problems. In such a setting, some will succeed and some will fail, but few will solve all the problems.

Those who do find the right answers won't share them with others. That would be cheating.

Suppose the teacher were to say, "I'm not testing you as individuals; I'm testing you as a class. Put your heads together and come up with the answers."

In all likelihood, no individual would possess **all** the knowledge needed to solve the problems or all the aptitude needed to apply the knowledge. But the class as a whole would have the knowledge and aptitude.

Communication and cooperation would spread the knowledge throughout the group, and the problems would be solved. Instead of some people succeeding and some failing, everyone would succeed.

What is traditionally known as cheating in the typical classroom is known as collaborative problem solving in the workplace.

That collaboration is the key to success in today's global economy.

THE IMPORTANCE OF TRUST

SEPTEMBER 25

Trust is the most valuable gift we can render to anyone.

We trust people, not machines or corporations, and trust must be built one person at a time—in business, relationships, and life.

An essential way to build trust is to stay in touch with people. So come up with a plan. Write or call three different people—a client, family member, or friend—at least once a day. That simple step lets them know they're on your mind—and also that you are on their minds.

Disagreements and misunderstandings enter any relationship, but don't let such obstacles torpedo the trust you've built up. Focus on fixing the problem and forget about fixing the blame.

One method to keep your relationships stable is to make a list of people with whom you've had a conflict. Once a year, approach these people and try to resolve the problem. Most people will respect you for doing that.

In our global economy, winners are those who know how to build long-term relationships with clients who'll give them repeat business and who'll recommend them to their friends.

The same goes for our life's journey. The more people we know and the smoother our relations with them, the greater our chances of finding true happiness.

THE OAR YOU NEED

SEPTEMBER 26

We all know them. And it may be you.

In a dead-end job. No chance for advancement. Playing it safe, resting on past achievements, staying with the familiar.

That's dangerous in today's world.

Any time we stop trying to get better, we're actually getting worse because we are living in an era of change. The comfortable environment in which we find ourselves could turn hostile overnight, or it could disappear altogether.

When we find ourselves in organizations that offer no more chance for progress or advancement, it's time to assess our options.

We could wait for the organization to change. We may even work within the organization to achieve that change. But when trapped in a static environment—no matter how pleasant it seems—it's time to look around for an exciting way out. Form a new vision and commit yourself to bringing it to reality.

Some people are happy with the challenges they encounter and the opportunities that beckon in their present positions. If you're in such a happy state, you don't have to leave. But remember that change is bound to come, and it's important to be prepared for it.

Keep abreast of developments in your field and related fields, and be prepared to change careers if necessary. Education is continual. Look upon it as the oar with which you can surely propel yourself through the seas of change.

THEREFORE, YOU ARE...WHAT?

SEPTEMBER 27

Sometimes we talk about success as if it were the end result of life's best journey, but that's not so.

Many people who make lots of money have asked, "If I'm so darned successful, why am I so miserable?"

When your life is merely successful but devoid of significance, you simply **can't** experience its fullness.

Success is secular by any measure; significance is spiritual by every measure. It's analogous to the difference between happiness and joy. You can be happy one moment and sad the next. But joy is something that lasts.

Similarly, success can turn to failure overnight. But significance sticks around for the long haul. Remember this: the significant thing is not what we do; it's what we are.

René Descartes, the French philosopher, proposed this formula: "I think, therefore I am."

One might extend that another step: "I am, therefore I do."

Too many people put that formula in reverse: "I do, therefore I am." What we **do** is a thing of the moment.

What we **are** is enduring.

YOUR MOST CONSTRUCTIVE HOUR OF THE DAY

SEPTEMBER 28

In his book *Charlie and the Chocolate Factory*, Roald Dahl wrote: "So please, oh PLEASE, we beg, we pray, go throw your TV set away, and in its place you can install, a lovely bookshelf on the wall."

Reading is one of the most efficient conduits to the mind. A daily habit of reading can help you build a refuge from the miseries in life or give you a road map to help you find direction, to focus, and to grow.

All you really need is an hour a day to read constructive material on a topic related to your areas of interest. You'll notice a change within a week.

Avoid television programs and movies that poison the mind with corruption, decadence, and violence. Cable and satellite channels are rich with programs on history, nature, and current events. Why contaminate the mind with useless content?

Avoid programs that have no social, educational, or spiritual value. They're like artificial sweeteners that satisfy the palate without adding nutritional value. It's been said that a hummingbird will sip artificially sweetened water as readily as it will drink water sweetened with sugar. But if it drinks the artificially sweetened water exclusively, the hummingbird runs out of energy and goes into a coma. Don't go into an intellectual or spiritual coma from feeding your mind on valueless content.

Books and the mass media are part of your environment. Be sure to make it a healthy, wholesome environment.

FIND YOUR TALENT

SEPTEMBER 29

You are a talented person. It would be tragic not to use your natural gifts. Clerical workers with a talent for writing can find rewarding careers in journalism, public relations, advertising, or as an author. Cab drivers with the gift of gab can become stand-up comics or actors. Sales clerks with minds like calculators could go into finance. The bartender who sketches on sandwich boards could work behind an easel rather than a bar tap.

There is nothing wrong with being a clerical worker, cab driver, sales clerk, or bartender if that's what you like and what you do well. But too many people drift into these jobs because they're the first things available. Then they get stuck in them because they never wake up to the marketplace value of their real talents.

Everyone is talented in something. Find your strong points, give them the recognition they deserve, and use them to do what you like to do.

DON'T SHOW OFF

SEPTEMBER 30

The purpose of communication is to convey ideas, not to show off your vocabulary.

The vocabulary you use in everyday speech has probably served you well. You use words you understand, and chances are, you use words your friends, family, and acquaintances understand.

If you try to use words beyond the vocabulary of people you're trying to communicate with, you're not communicating. You're showing off.

To see the power of simplicity, read the Gettysburg Address, the Sermon on the Mount, or poetry from Billy Collins, the former Poet Laureate of the United States.

Take the first four lines from Collins's poem "Winter Syntax."

> *A sentence starts out like a lone traveler*
> *heading into a blizzard at midnight,*
> *tilting into the wind, one arm shielding his face,*
> *the tails of his thin coat flapping behind him.*

No big words there.

Communication that endures is communication written in plain, simple language.

OCTOBER

THE HEAVEN OF A GOAL

OCTOBER 1

More than a century ago, English poet Robert Browning wrote, "Ah, but a man's reach should exceed his grasp, Or what's a heaven for?"

If you follow Browning's philosophy, you're going to need a heaven because your earthly life is going to be full of frustration. Achieving your goals is one of the most enriching experiences of life. Individual goals are very personal things, and only you can decide whether your goals are high enough for you.

A good goal will make you stretch, but it won't cause you to break.

What goals have you set for yourself?

SIX STEPS FOR YOU

OCTOBER 2

As you begin your day, think about these six steps to success:

1. Decide what you want in life. Identify the things you do well and that you enjoy doing.
2. Create a vision of success, and make a commitment to achieve it. A commitment is like your signature on a contract.
3. Draw up a plan for achieving your dream. Don't ask, "Can I do it?" Ask, "How can I do it?" Be guided by what is possible.
4. Once you know where you want to go, prepare yourself for the journey.Acquire the physical, mental/emotional, social and spiritual balance you'll need to stay motivated and keep you on course.
5. Execute your plan in three phases: action, learning, and applying. Ask yourself what must be done next to achieve your goals. You'll never know whether a specific action will be successful until you've tried it and observed the results. This will enable you to learn what works and what doesn't. Use your mistakes as lessons, and apply what you learn to implementation of the plan.
6. When you've achieved the last goal in your action plan, create a new vision, make a new commitment, and start the process anew.

Success builds upon success. There's no magic in it. The power is in you.

YOUR LIFE: CHECK IT OUT

OCTOBER 3

If someone handed you an envelope and told you it contained $1,000 all in $100 bills, would you hand it back to them and say, "Sure doesn't feel like $1,000"?

No, you'd open it. You have to take the same approach with your life. Look. Listen. Take action.

Start with the words you use. Remove the words *should* and *if* from your vocabulary and replace them with the word *how*. You choose what you want to **do**, whether it is a new job, hobby, or outlook in life.

To get there, create a to-do list. Nothing big. Just something manageable. Now the fun starts. Be enthusiastic. Tell others what you want to do. Start small and get started. You'll be surprised what you'll find.

You'll feel a little like Leonardo da Vinci. "It had long since come to my attention that people of accomplishment rarely sat back and let things happen to them," he once said. "They went out and happened to things."

With life, **don't** be a bystander.

LEARN FROM SEQUOYAH

OCTOBER 4

Sequoyah, the great Cherokee leader—a sorcerer? At one time, the Cherokees thought he was.

After the War of 1812, when Sequoyah had served three months in the American Army, he went back to his work as a silversmith and came up with eighty-five symbols that could be used to form words.

The Cherokee didn't trust what they saw—and believed. They declared Sequoyah a sorcerer, and he and his first student, his daughter, were taken to trial.

But by the trial's end, Cherokee warriors had become his students, and within a week, they were able to read and write in their own language. Soon, a large part of the Cherokee Nation achieved literacy and helped to preserve their history, culture, and spiritual practices.

Sometimes being a leader is easier said than done because leaders must:

- help people decide for themselves what to do.
- expect excellence in those around them and make those expectations known.
- invite people to speak up, and listen and respond to those who do.
- welcome both good news and bad news, knowing they can't lead wisely unless they're fully informed.
- believe in themselves.
- trust their own sense of direction.

As Texas statesman Sam Houston once said, "Your invention of the alphabet is worth more to your people than two bags full of gold in the hands of every Cherokee."

YOU'RE MORE THAN A COMPUTER: BE CREATIVE

OCTOBER 5

The future belongs to those who create it. And that means you.

If you expect to share in the fruits of innovation and change, you must become an agent of change. That means you must become something a computer can never become—a creative force.

Creative people never become married to an idea because if it leads to a dead end, they'll look for another creative direction. They have a thirst for knowledge so they like to read, travel, and explore and believe time is well spent when browsing through libraries and surfing the Internet to read a favorite blog.

They look at the future as a big adventure instead of a looming threat because they're not afraid to bid good-bye to the status quo and embrace new practices.

And they're eager to seize the opportunities the future brings and turn challenges into triumphs.

Computers can never do that.

Computers are wonderful tools for performing calculations, accumulating data, and facilitating communication. But they are incapable of original thought and original action. They are strictly dependent on human input.

Creative people make good use of computers. But computers will never be able to lead or inspire, or to duplicate the accomplishments of creative people.

But you can.

NEVER STOP

OCTOBER 6

It's been said that education is what you have left after you've forgotten everything you've learned.

In a sense, people in today's workplace must constantly forget everything they know.

Several years ago, the *Wall Street Journal* estimated that product generations often last less than eighteen months. Some entire product lines turn over every year, some in six months.

That was so different more than a century ago when Henry Ford rode to success by finding a product that worked and turned it out year after year with only minor change. Today, a company that does that will quickly roll off a cliff called obsolescence.

The companies that roll to success are those that develop constant learning capacities and exploit them.

Learning has to become a renewable resource. As a spring replenishes itself when water is withdrawn, educated individuals replenish their learning when existing knowledge has served its purpose.

Think of the art of learning like a water dipper. When the water is gone, the dipper can't refill itself.

French composer Michel Legrand knows that. He said: "The more I live, the more I learn. The more I learn, the more I realize, the less I know."

THE BABE'S CLAIM

OCTOBER 7

It was game three of the 1932 World Series, and Babe Ruth was up to bat. He had two strikes against him when he pointed toward center field.

On the next pitch, a curve ball, Babe sent the ball flying into the section of the stands where he had pointed. Imagine how he would have felt had he struck out.

Babe had given himself a task and, before thousands of fans, had made a commitment to accomplish it. He now had all the more reason to do what he had set out to do.

People can dawdle in their careers until they decide what they want to accomplish and keep that goal constantly in front of their eyes. Some put the goal in writing and tape it to their mirrors. Others put it elsewhere to be constantly reminded of it.

The most effective incentive to succeed comes when you've announced your goals to all. You know what you expect to accomplish. In effect, you call your own shots.

It worked for Babe Ruth. It will work for you.

THE NEED FOR ROL

OCTOBER 8

Truly successful people know that there's something more important than ROI, or return on investment. It's "ROL"—return on life.

ROI is what we get back from investing money; ROL is what we get back from investing ourselves.

Here's a good formula for achieving balance in life:

- Invest a third of your life in earning; you must have resources if you want to be able to give resources.
- Invest a third of your life in learning; read books and periodicals every week.
- Invest a third of your life in giving and serving.

Cultivate a love for learning and a capacity for earning. These qualities are important ingredients for success, significance, and fulfillment. But the things people really get passionate about are the things that come directly from their sense of service.

Some people lead their lives a task at a time without meditating on where the series of tasks is taking them. Some live at the goal level, aiming toward short-term objectives without thinking of the big picture. But the happiest people are those who live their lives at the purpose level.

Find a purpose larger than you and invest yourself in it. You'll be gratified at the return on life that it yields.

That is ROL. When you're balanced, you don't wait for opportunities to serve your friend, your neighbor, someone you don't know. You look for them.

CHANGE HEARTS AND MINDS

OCTOBER 9

T oday, see yourself as a transformative leader.

Put emphasis on what people become and equip them with the tools to acquire knowledge on their own. You'll change minds, inspire positive attitudes, and create the kind of atmosphere that makes people want to change.

They'll respect you. And if people respect you, they'll be willing to follow you.

Willingness to do a job comes from attitudes, not orders.

Dedication or a person's pride in quality are not skills. They are attitudes, and transformational leaders can help instill those attitudes through their own appearance and confidence.

When you spot a problem, don't go looking for someone to blame. Go look for a solution. Encourage others to offer ideas, listen to what others say, and empower others to act on their own initiative. When they have offered an idea, don't ridicule it.

Learn from failure. Don't hog the glory; spread it around. If you do that, people will feel ownership in a project and invest themselves in it.

When that happens, you won't simply change behavior. You'll change hearts and minds.

DON'T BE A PRISONER TO YOUR MISTAKES

OCTOBER 10

Mistakes will come. Don't fear them. Take this advice from Benjamin Franklin: "You will know failure. Continue to reach out."

Better yet, move forward a few centuries and heed what evangelical minister Rick Warren has to say: "We are products of our past, but we don't have to be prisoners of it." We all can learn from our mistakes. To make that happen, follow these suggestions:

- ☼ **Have measurable goals.** You won't know whether you're moving toward your goals unless you have some way of measuring the motion. That's why your goals should be specific.
- ☼ **Seek positive and negative feedback.** Encourage those you trust to give both legitimate criticism and earned recognition.

The greatest enemy of your creative powers is smug complacency. Never be satisfied with less than what you are capable of doing.

That's what leads to true happiness.

YOUR OWN PERSONAL MARATHON
OCTOBER 11

The road to success is not a meandering path. It's a carefully planned route. But planning a route only tells you where you expect to go.

Getting there requires you to hit the road—or lace up your running shoes. Think of it like a road race.

If you're running the marathon and you go all-out for the first mile, you may take the lead, but victory ultimately will go to the runner who strikes the most sustainable pace.

If the pace is too slow, others will pass you. If it's too fast, you'll run out of energy before you reach the end of the race.

A marathon runner's objective is not to lead after the first mile, or even after the first twenty-five miles. It's to finish the entire twenty-six miles. The successful runner, fueled by his own endorphins—or "runner's high"—will find his pace and feel like he can go on forever.

You need to strike that kind of balance in your personal habits and behavior. Find the happy medium between minimum performance and a breakneck pace that only leads to burnout. Then you're ready.

Once the action has begun, you'll feel it. A motivational edge will take root in your heart and soul and give you the adrenaline to carry your action plan to a successful conclusion.

DON'T SQUANDER TIME

OCTOBER 12

What would you do if someone gave you a million dollars? The first thing you'd probably do is protect it. You certainly wouldn't leave it in clear view on the front seat of your car. And you wouldn't break it up into small bills and hand it out to everybody you met.

But isn't it ironic that some people protect their money and possessions, yet let their lives slip away with little thought?

They don't seem to realize that time is their most valuable possession. Each of us is given 1,440 minutes each day, and no one has more time than you do.

Every minute is precious. Cherish it. Invest it. Use it to do more, grow more, give more, and be more.

OUT OF THE FIRE

OCTOBER 13

A group hiking through the mountains once found themselves engulfed by smoke from a forest fire. The fire threatened to encircle them. The smoke obscured all landmarks. They began to stumble in all directions until one of them said confidently, "Follow me."

Linking hands to stay together, they followed the leader. She led them on a straight path through the smoke to safety.

"How did you know the way out?" one of the hikers asked later.

"I didn't," she said, "but I knew we were goners if we didn't get out of there, so I set a course and stuck to it."

The leader had no more knowledge and skill than any of the other hikers. What she had was self-confidence.

U.S. General George Patton described it this way: "The most vital quality a soldier can possess is self-confidence."

DON'T BE AFRAID TO JUMP
OCTOBER 14

Many pilots have died because they stayed with their disabled aircraft too long and never ejected and parachuted away from danger. They preferred the familiarity of the cockpit even though it had become a death trap.

Many people have seen their careers crash because they preferred familiar but deadly old ways to the risky but rewarding new ways.

They never learned that standing still is really standing down. Look around you. We are living in an age where the dominant characteristic is change. When you see your present situation leveling off and beginning a downward trend, it's time to pull the cord.

Abandon the old career cockpit and eject into a new environment that offers challenge and excitement.

BUILDING BRIDGES

OCTOBER 15

C ommunication is at the heart of everything we do.

It is the foundation for interaction among human beings. Communication has to do with meaning, with understanding feelings, desires, needs, and ideas. Our world is filled with information.

But the greatest need is for understanding—for building bridges across the mental and emotional distances that separate individuals so we can better live, work, and get along together, making this earth the best possible home for the human race.

Sometimes, that may seem impossible.

But remember what Simone de Beauvoir, a French writer and philosopher, once said: "The fact that we are human beings is infinitely more important than all the peculiarities that distinguish human beings from one another."

Well said.

DOG DAYS

OCTOBER 16

Other animals respond to innate drives, but humans have the capacity to make ethical and moral judgments. Call it conscience, values, or whatever you will, something in all of us rises up at times and says, "This is good!" or "This is bad!"

We ignore our conscience to our own peril. According to German philosopher Jean-Jacques Rousseau, the conscience is "the voice of the soul." It is our divining rod to help us find what is right and true within us.

Irish playwright George Bernard Shaw once wrote, "A Native American elder once described his own inner struggles in this manner: Inside of me there are two dogs. One of the dogs is mean and evil. The other dog is good. The mean dog fights the good dog all the time. When asked which dog wins, he reflected for a moment and replied, 'The one I feed the most.'"

Make sure you feed the right one.

SIMPLE LITTLE WORDS

OCTOBER 17

It's one thing to know a lot of words. It's something else to be able to use them to inform, inspire, and influence people.

Parrots know words, but they can't use them to influence human conduct. You don't have to be a walking dictionary to be able to influence people.

Read the Sermon on the Mount and see how many big words you find in it. You'll find it in the book of Matthew, starting at chapter 5, verse 2. It begins:

And He began to teach them. He said:
Blessed are the poor in spirit, for theirs is the kingdom of heaven.
Blessed are those who mourn, for they will be comforted.
Blessed are the meek, for they will inherit the earth.

Jesus's Sermon on the Mount goes on for another two chapters, outlining the morals and values for mankind. The greatest truths are usually expressed in the simplest language.

ADD THE COLOR OF ENTHUSIASM
OCTOBER 18

To comprehend enthusiasm, imagine an artist doing a pencil sketch of a beautiful pastoral scene at sunset. When the sketch is completed, it is proportionally correct, exact in detail, and sharp in contrast.

But it is dull and uninteresting because it lacks color, shading, and warmth. Now the skilled artist takes brushes and plays light against shadows, adds colors and hues, and paints in depth and feeling.

Suddenly the picture comes alive.

Enthusiasm is the color of inspiration and courage. It is the light of creativity and insight. It is the depth of emotion and the feeling of purpose.

Enthusiastic people experience life from the inside out, and their enthusiasm makes things happen; it gets people's attention in a gracious and polite way, and it persuades people to take notice, even follow.

That is a color we all need.

MAKE IT QUICK

OCTOBER 19

Successful people don't lie awake at night agonizing over decisions and directions. They're quick to decide and slow to change their minds. Unsuccessful people are often slow to decide and quick to change their minds.

The difference lies in the fact that successful people are guided by a set of constant principles. They make decisions that are in harmony with these principles. Therefore, their decisions are as solid as their principles. They don't second-guess themselves and seldom reverse themselves.

Remember what former President Harry Truman said: "All my life, whenever it comes time to make a decision, I make it and forget about it."

ACT NOW
OCTOBER 20

The time to act is now. You can't start tomorrow and you can't start "someday." "Someday" is usually a euphemism for "never." Milestones are achieved one step at a time. So decide what the first step will be and take it.

And remember, don't mistake the difficult for the impossible.

Inch by inch, life is a cinch. Big achievements often start with small steps. The key is to do something.

Now. Today.

THE SUCCESS OF FAILURE

OCTOBER 21

H is name is Blake, and once again, he was bypassed for another promotion after twenty years on the job. His boss saw it differently. He told Blake that he had one year of experience twenty times.

"You haven't learned from the mistakes you have made," Blake's boss said. "You're still making the same mistakes you made during your first year here."

Blake had not learned an essential truth involved in success: a productive failure is more valuable than a nonproductive success.

A productive failure is one where you learn something that will help you build toward success. A nonproductive success is one you achieve without knowing how you achieved it. It teaches you nothing.

A basketball player named Michael knows that well.

I've missed more than nine thousand shots in my career. I've lost almost three hundred games. Twenty-six times, I've been trusted to take the game's winning shot and missed. I've failed over, *and over*, and over again in my life. And that is why I succeed.

That player was Michael Jordan.

CONGRATULATE YOURSELF

OCTOBER 22

When something good happens to a friend, you're probably quick to congratulate. You should be your own best friend.

When something good happens to **you**, why not congratulate yourself? You might even arrange some sort of celebration.

Consider what Maxwell Maltz, an American cosmetic surgeon, once said: "If you make friends with yourself, you will never be alone."

Or maybe it'll remind you of something we all have read from Theodor Geisel, better known as Dr. Seuss: "Today you are You, that is truer than true. There is no one alive who is Youer than You."

Provide a pleasant incentive to go out and repeat your good fortune. When you acknowledge a special achievement, you give yourself a boost toward the next one and provide the energy to pursue your dream.

BE THE CAPTAIN OF YOU

OCTOBER 23

Disguising incompetence doesn't alter the basic condition. But incompetence can be overcome.

If you're in a job that requires talents you don't possess, don't spend your time covering up your lack of talent. Spend it looking for a job that will enable you to use the talents you **do** have.

Think about William Ernest Henley. He didn't have a lack of talent. He had the lack of a leg. At age twelve, he lost one of his legs right below the knee because of tubercular arthritis. He went on to become an editor, critic, and poet who excelled at his craft. More than a century ago he wrote, "I am the master of my fate, I am the captain of my soul."

Fourteen words to live by.

FIND NEW FRIENDS

OCTOBER 24

S ome people sap your self-confidence, and some leave you with feelings of self-doubt. Yet others give you strength and build your self-confidence.

It may be surprising to notice that the people who sap your belief in yourself are not the truly great people around you. They are the small-minded individuals who are always complaining. Generally, those who might have reason to belittle your abilities are the very ones who are most apt to encourage you to try.

For example, meet humorist Joe Larson, who said, "My friends didn't believe that I could become a successful speaker. So I did something about it. I went out and found me some new friends!"

Occasionally, we all need to do the same.

LOMBARDI'S SECRET

OCTOBER 25

When Vince Lombardi took over the Green Bay Packers football team at age forty-five, he found a defeated, disheartened group of men ready to quit. In the preceding season, they had won only two games.

Yet three years later, they won the world professional football championship and went on to become what many sportswriters have called "football's greatest dynasty."

What made the difference? Lombardi's message was clear: we're going to get back to basics and win!

In every line of endeavor, there are certain basics that must be mastered. Execute them well, and you're on your way to success. This applies whether you're a team leader attempting to inspire success in your fellow workers, a salesperson trying to persuade prospects to buy, or a chief executive officer working to rally an entire company around a vision for the future.

It matters little what you are undertaking, what types of people you deal with, what kind of personality you have, or what kind of economic situation you face. Certain principles are always at work in the process.

Understand and master those principles, and you can be a winner.

THE POWER OF OBSERVATION

OCTOBER 26

Y ou can't describe something you haven't seen, and you haven't really seen something until you've examined it carefully. Therefore, a good communicator must be a keen observer.

The poet Robert Frost was a meticulous observer. "The Vermont mountains stretch extended straight," he wrote. "New Hampshire mountains curl up in a coil."

Who but a person intimately acquainted with the New England landscape could have written that description?

"Like a piece of ice on a hot stove, the poem must ride on its own melting," he wrote in a preface to his collected poems.

Frost had not only seen ice melting on a hot stove, he had keenly observed it.

And Frost had seen birch trees in winter "bend to left and right. Across the lines of straighter darker trees." In his poem "Birches," he observed:

> *Often you must have seen them*
> *Loaded with ice on a sunny winter morning*
> *After a rain. They click upon themselves*
> *As the breeze rises, and turn many-colored*
> *As the stir cracks and crazes their enamel.*

Frost's close observation enabled him to paint a word picture of the birch trees, coated with ice that broke off under the sun's warmth into shattered shells that resembled piles of broken glass.

Look around you. Go beyond seeing. Start observing.

ACCEPT THE GIFT OF THE MOMENT

OCTOBER 27

The pessimist has screened out all of the exciting gifts that the present moment promises to bring, while the optimist is ready and eager to receive those gifts.

The pessimist is either longing for a better moment, which may come someday, or reliving a more pleasant moment that is long gone.

But optimists are willing to trust in their plans for the future and in their ability to carry them out. They are willing to savor the memories of the past. Most of all, though, they are alert to the opportunities that each moment has to give.

Optimism is a gift to appreciate and behold. Receive it. Treasure it. Use it.

THE PATIENT LUMBERJACK
OCTOBER 28

Two men were out in the forest spending their day chopping wood. One took no breaks and only thirty minutes for lunch, while the other took several breaks and even a short nap after lunch. By day's end, the man who took no breaks looked at his friend's woodpile and got angry.

His buddy, the lumberjack who took a nap at lunch, had cut more wood than he had.

"How did you cut more wood than me?" he asked. "Every time I looked around you were sitting down!"

"That's true," his friend responded. "But didn't you notice that while I was sitting down, I was sharpening my ax?"

What you can draw from this story is how you can pace your life:

- Take a short relaxation or meditation break periodically to recharge.
- Vary your tasks from time to time. Working too long in a single position or one task will reduce your productivity and cause stress.
- Exercise every day. That'll relieve tension and you'll sleep better.
- Practice emptying your mind each night as you prepare for bed.

Remind yourself that you have done all you could that day, and prepare for the next.

THREE CHARACTERISTICS FOR YOU

OCTOBER 29

The world doesn't need more managers. It needs more leaders. A manager manages **things**. A leader leads **people**.

A manager tries to keep things running smoothly and not alter the status quo. A leader is constantly looking for ways to change the status quo, charting new paths and encouraging others to want to follow them.

Leaders come in every walk of life. But they have three basic characteristics:

1. They don't tell people what to do; they help people decide for themselves what to do.
2. They expect excellence in those around them and make those expectations known. The people they lead will usually live up to these expectations.
3. They invite people to speak up, and they listen and respond to those who do. They welcome good news and bad news from their associates, knowing that they can't lead wisely unless they're fully informed.

Embrace these characteristics. You'll feel it in your heart and soul. That is the font from which leadership springs.

If you have it, you'll know it. Others will too.

TRUTHS THAT WILL NEVER CHANGE

OCTOBER 30

John Donne could preach.

In the seventeenth century, he was known for fiery sermons that were full of imagery and dazzling wordplay. But Donne was also a poet—and considered the greatest of the metaphysical poets, a group of talented wordsmiths who wrote in the first person about emotions and feelings. Here is a great example from Donne:

> No man is an island, entire of itself; every man is a piece of the continent; a part of the main. If a clod be washed away by the sea, Europe is the less, as well as if a promontory were, as well as if a manor of thy friends, or of thine own were; any man's death diminishes me, because I am involved in mankind; and therefore never send to know for whom the bell tolls; it tolls for thee.

These truths do not change. They were valid when your grandparents lived, and they will be valid for generations to come. They are our guides to future happiness, and their value exceeds that of anything that has emerged from California's Silicon Valley or lecture halls near the Charles River in Boston.

In an age in which most things that glitter are plastic, they are nuggets of gold.

Like these fifteen words that Jesus said: "As ye would that men should do to you, do ye also to them likewise."

Timeless words. Advice for the ages. Embrace it.

FIND YOUR JOY

OCTOBER 31

If you want the kind of happiness and deep personal satisfaction out of life that circumstances cannot **destroy**, do this: search until you find what you can do best, what no one could pay you enough money not to do, and what you would gladly pay for the privilege of doing.

Then do it with all that is within you.

One high school teacher did that. He liked to teach. But he loved to write. He supplemented his teaching income by writing short stories and later writing a novel about a teenager with psychic powers, a perfect story for any Halloween.

The teacher threw it in the trash. But his wife retrieved it and encouraged him to finish it. He did. The book was *Carrie*, and the former high school teacher is Stephen King.

Since then, he has written more than fifty novels—and still counting. Here's how he describes his career:

Yes, I've made a great deal of dough from my fiction, but I never set a single word down on paper with the thought of being paid for it... I have written because it fulfilled me... I did it for the buzz, I did it for the pure joy of the thing. And if you can do it for joy, you can do it forever.

NOVEMBER

ARREST YOUR TIME ROBBER

NOVEMBER 1

W e all hate procrastination. But here are some tips for dealing with it:

- ⚙ Get ready for the next day before you go to sleep.
- ⚙ Get a good night's sleep.
- ⚙ Listen to your alarm clock. Hear it, get up, and start your routine.
- ⚙ Exercise first thing. That'll get you ready for the entire day.
- ⚙ Greet the day in a way that appeals to you. Find a pattern that suits you and stick to it.
- ⚙ Take some time early to get in touch with your inner self. Do something that fills your mind with positive thoughts before it has time to run into the problems of the day.
- ⚙ Have your whole day planned and stick to the plan. Map out your day by writing down your tasks. Even if you have to set aside your plans several times a day, it's better than wondering what you will have to do next.

It's really all about self-discipline—about seeing what you have to do and getting it done rather than putting it off.

It's like that old saying about the bullfrog. "If you must swallow a bullfrog, don't look at him too long, lest he become too big for you to swallow."

And no one wants that to happen.

AMPLIFY YOUR ATTITUDE

NOVEMBER 2

A positive attitude is like love in at least one respect: the more you give, the more you get.

It does you absolutely no good to harbor all those good feelings inside yourself. The strength of a positive attitude comes from spreading it around.

Think of a time when you have helped someone see the positive side of a problem. Didn't you feel good about being able to help out?

Sometimes an encouraging word is the best help you can offer to someone. So don't disregard the power of sharing positive thinking.

Find a deserving soul today and lift them up.

SELF-UNDERSTANDING IS STRENGTH

NOVEMBER 3

The most important person for you to understand is yourself. Here are three rules to follow as you commune with your inner self daily:

- ⚙ Identify your weaknesses and shore them up.
- ⚙ Analyze the way you think, respond, and act.
- ⚙ Learn what your strengths are and exert them positively.

If you do these things, personal success will follow. Just as day follows night.

LAUGH, LAUGH, LAUGH

NOVEMBER 4

N othing softens the challenges of life like a good sense of humor. How often have you had an experience that you considered humiliating, mortifying, and even degrading at the time, but that you were later able to tell about with laughter?

If it's funny in retrospect, why wasn't it funny at the time? The answer is in your reaction to it.

If you can learn to look for the humor at the time of the experience, you'll save yourself a lot of emotional pain, and you'll cause other people to be more comfortable around you.

It really is all a matter of perspective.

THE IMPORTANCE OF POSITION

NOVEMBER 5

Don't be a promoter. Promoters promise.

If you want to improve your reputation, don't promise—demonstrate.

You want people to benefit in a very valuable way from knowing, interacting, and doing business with you. You want people to perceive that working with you will be good for their business.

Position yourself as a person or company with solutions to problems people are worried about. Clients will pay attention when you help them get what they want from life. Your major goal should be to create results. That makes you valuable.

Have a clear vision and a solid strategy that maps out how you are going to follow through. Connect with your contacts on a daily basis. Send something to your most important contacts monthly to let them know you are thinking of them. Employ the generosity factor. If you see a book you like, buy a few copies and send it to your clients.

Look for ways you can serve your community—not because you want people to see how great you are, but because you want to improve the world you share with others.

A HITCHHIKING PERSPECTIVE FOR YOU

NOVEMBER 6

I f your action plan calls for hitchhiking across Europe to acquire an international perspective, your grandfather might think that outlandishly impractical. From his perspective, your time might be better spent acquiring experience and seniority in a job at home.

But your grandfather grew up in a more stable business climate, where it was reasonable to expect to stay with the same company, on the same career track, for most of your working life. From a twenty-first-century perspective, that may not be a reasonable prospect at all.

A global perspective may be more important than a couple of years of experience. You'll have to make that decision in the light of your vision, values, and goals.

Thomas Francine did just that. For three years, from 2008 to 2011, he hitchhiked through thirty-four states and thirteen countries, from Denmark to Turkey, and produced a thirty-minute documentary, *The Greater Good: A Hitchhike Perspective.*

During a 2013 TED Talk, Francine said, "The world may be a lot better than you realize. And you can work with the good and make it better in simple ways."

That's not your grandfather talking. What Francine found on his travels opened his eyes to finding new ideas, issues, and solutions.

You can do that too.

IMAGINE YOUR POTENTIAL

NOVEMBER 7

E ven before he walked up to the green, world champion golfer Jack Nicklaus always imagined it in his head.

"I never hit a shot, not even in practice, without having a very sharp in-focus picture of it in my head," he once said.

You can do that too. The idea of visualizing, or mental rehearsing, can improve your game, your performance, or simply who you are.

Researchers at Ohio University found that volunteers were able to increase their muscle strength simply by imagining using the muscles.

It works because neural networks in your brain tell your muscles what to do, as if you had physically performed the activity. Our brains don't know the difference between real and imagined.

Mental rehearsal can also prepare you for potential obstacles in your job or your life. After anticipating issues, you can imagine yourself handling them smoothly and confidently, thereby reducing anxiety and improving self-confidence.

Be like Jack Nicklaus on the green. Use your mind and rehearse. And see what happens.

THE BENEFITS OF STRONG RELATIONSHIPS
NOVEMBER 8

In the world of business—and in the business of life—you need to remember that building relationships is a key to success and your own happiness.

Take Lee Iacocca. When he took control of the Chrysler Corporation, one of his first moves was to dismiss the two advertising agencies that were handling the Chrysler account, replacing them with the agency he had worked with so successfully as president of Ford.

As Iacocca put it, he didn't have enough time to acclimate Chrysler's agencies to his way of thinking. It was much simpler for him to bring along an agency he had worked with before. Iacocca's decision resulted in the largest single transfer of an advertising account ever recorded—$50 million.

That agency had become much more to Iacocca than just another advertising company. To Iacocca, it was an indispensable ally—and a valuable consulting resource—and it paid off handsomely in the long run.

When it comes to building relationships, it's not just about money. Studies show you can live longer, be healthier, and handle stress more effectively with strong social connections.

But it takes work. You need to listen effectively, give people your time, trust more, develop empathy and your communication skills, and learn how to give—and take—feedback.

As actress Susan Sarandon said, "When you start to develop your powers of empathy and imagination, the whole world opens up to you."

Imagine that.

CLIMBING OUT OF A RUT

NOVEMBER 9

S ome people dream exciting **dreams** but never bring them out of dreamland because they often mistake an exciting dream for an impossible one.

There's an unconscious rating process that we go through when we're sizing up tasks. We all do it. We think of the task in comparison to our own capacities.

Look at it this way: If we think the task is bigger than we are, we become discouraged and don't try. If we think the task is beneath our capacities, we're bored by it and bypass it. But if we think the task matches our capacities, we're likely to wade into it.

The key to motivating yourself is to upgrade your estimate of your own capacities by doing this: if the dream excites you, tell yourself you can achieve it, because if it were beyond your **reach**, it wouldn't excite you.

The next time you face a major challenge, give your estimate of your capabilities an upward revision. That'll help you get out of your life's rut.

People stay in ruts because it takes less effort to follow the rut than to get out of it. But when the pain of staying in the rut becomes appreciably greater than the pain of getting out of it, you'll leave.

If you do **that**, your dreams **won't** remain out of reach.

THE MUSIC INSIDE
NOVEMBER 10

K en Helser is an excellent musician. He plays piano. And he once used his talents for a different kind of audience.

He played for prisoners.

He played all over the southeast. Yet it wasn't the music he played. It was the words he chose.

"When I was a young boy, I was given a little xylophone for Christmas," he told inmates. "With it came a set of instructions. I was well on the way to learning how to play it when I lost the instruction booklet."

After he and his parents had searched the house, the yard, and the family car, all to no avail, he sat down and began to cry.

"Mother," he whined, "the music's gone!"

"No, son" his mother replied, "the instructions are gone. The music is inside you. Listen to it, and you can play it."

After that story, Helser told the prisoners the kicker: "Here in prison, you may feel cut off from everything, like life is closing in on you, and like the music is gone from your life. But the music's inside you; if you listen to it, you can play it."

Remember, you are a bundle of potential. All you need to do is convince yourself. You can do it. Tell yourself that—over and over.

ALWAYS REMEMBER

NOVEMBER 11

Doc Long laid on a battlefield for eighteen hours outside the tiny town of Ancerville in France during World War II.

Snow fell, the temperature dropped, the blood from his wound turned to a trickle, and afternoon became night. Doc started to pray.

A French soldier rescued him, and several days later he was given the items that were cut from his body. He had his wallet and his Bible from Aunt May that he kept over his heart.

His Bible had been pierced by a piece of shrapnel, possibly from a mortar shell. His Bible saved his life.

These are the type of stories we need to remember to honor our veterans. Take a moment **today**—in prayer, in conversation, or just in silent meditation—to thank our veterans.

Patriotism is a value to cherish, and our military deserves our respect and admiration for their dedication and their sacrifice. They embody the very essence of service, honor, and leadership.

On a cold day in a veterans' cemetery, Long told his story in front of a crowd huddled in coats. He came wearing a reproduction of a World War II brown wool uniform and looked like an old warrior with a white broom of a moustache.

With the help of his cane, Long walked to the podium and spoke for twenty minutes about why he fought and what kept him alive on a battlefield more than seventy years ago, far from home.

"We did not fight because we waited for what was in front of us," he said. "We fought because we loved what was behind us."

FRIENDS WON'T LET YOU BE SLOPPY

NOVEMBER 12

When we have not done our best—and we know it—it hurts to hear someone we love say they know we could have done better. Yet our real friends are the ones who won't let us get away with sloppy work or halfhearted efforts.

Gently—ever so gently—they tell us that they expected better from us. These criticisms, in their own way, are actually compliments. Constructive criticism, when graciously accepted, can improve our performance while helping us build self-confidence.

It shows us that we really can do better.

GET RID OF THE PAST

NOVEMBER 13

When you decide to buy all new furniture for your home, what do you have to do? You probably have to get rid of most of your old furniture. Otherwise, there won't be room for the new.

The same thing is true of new ideas and new ways of doing things. Before you can make significant changes, you have to get rid of the old ways.

Forget old resentments. Let go of the ideas and habits you've grown comfortable with and explore new trends, technology, and opportunities that spark your own inspiration.

Dee Hock, the founder and former CEO of the Visa Credit Card Association, sees it this way:

The problem is never how to get new, innovative thoughts into your mind, but how to get old ones out. Every mind is a room filled with archaic furniture. Make an empty space in any corner of your mind, and creativity will instantly fill it.

FIND YOUR PLAN B

NOVEMBER 14

It always helps to have a Plan B, but it should be designed to take you toward the same goal you set for Plan A.

You'll be able to stay with a task for the duration if you think it through before you undertake it. So consider some rules to follow:

- Examine the probable impact of each action you take.
- Think about how it will affect the goals you've set.
- Try to anticipate the things that might go wrong.
- Then, develop strategies for dealing with them.

Don't think of it as a failure to have to rely on a Plan B. James Altucher, author of *Choose Yourself*, believes the same thing. He wrote:

It's the BEGINNING of success when you start having multiple plans. Life is not a bullet going in a straight line but a scattershot that hits every possible future.

DUNG = DOLLARS

NOVEMBER 15

Richard and Horace Waybright, along with their sons, run the Mason Dixon Farm near Gettysburg, Pennsylvania. It's been in their family since the 1700s, and like many farmers, the Waybright brothers wrestled with the rising costs of feeding and taking care of 2,400 head of cattle.

That's where the cow manure comes in.

To counteract the increasing cost of electricity as well as to find ways to dispose of their cattle's waste, they constructed a power generator that uses methane gas produced by heated cow manure from their herd.

Farmers around the Mason Dixon Farm made fun of it. They called the project "Waybright's Folly." But the generator cut their annual power bill from $30,000 to $15,000.

Soon farmers, members of Congress, and agriculture ministers from around the world came to the Waybright farm to see how it was done.

The response shouldn't surprise anyone. The Waybrights say they had one of the first milking parlors in the country. The generator simply fits into the family's entrepreneurial spirit.

Just look at the farm's motto: "Change is inevitable. Success is optional."

WATCH THAT OWL

NOVEMBER 16

Once, at a church meeting, a longtime deacon listened to the arguments about buying a new chandelier and rose to have his say.

"Brethren," he began, "I'm firmly opposed to this church spending its money on a chandelier, for three solid reasons: first, nobody in the church knows how to spell it; second, nobody here can play it; and third, what this church needs is more light."

Another time at a barbershop, a man who fancied himself as an authority on everything walked in and saw a scruffy owl perched on top of a cabinet. The man began to belittle the taxidermist for doing such a poor job of stuffing the bird and held court from a nearby chair on the finer points of ornithology.

"The owl's wings are at the wrong angle, and look at that head, it's tilted all wrong," he told the crowd around him. "And color of the feathers? Well, I think that taxidermist used some cheap hair color. That's what I think!"

When the man finished, everyone in the barbershop looked at the owl. The bird blinked a couple of times, stretched its wings, and flew to the opposite side of the room.

Both stories illustrate the truth of the adage: it's better for people to wonder why you didn't talk rather than for them to wonder why you did.

HARD LESSONS FROM THE HIGH SEAS

NOVEMBER 17

The NS *Savannah* was one beautiful ship. So was the SS *United States*.

The Savannah was the world's first nuclear-powered merchant ship. The United States set records crossing the Atlantic. Both ships were superbly designed and technological marvels.

But disputes with maritime unions over the manning of the *Savannah* led to its early retirement. The launch of the SS *United States* came at the dawn of the jet age, making it obsolete.

All that quality, wasted. Communications can be like that.

They may sound good to the ear or look good to the eye. But if they accomplish nothing, the care that goes into them is lavished in vain.

What about the NS *Savannah* and the SS *United States*? Today, the SS *United States* is lashed to a dock just south of downtown Philadelphia, and the NS *Savannah* is tucked behind a grain elevator at a pier along Baltimore's waterfront.

Both ships are nowhere bound.

MAKE THAT "TO BE" LIST

NOVEMBER 18

We've all run into people who are constantly late or absent from work, don't push themselves, or feel fatigued constantly by keeping up with the pace of life. They have TGIF—the Thank God It's Friday blues. But every day can be Friday if you work at it.

The bottom line is this: what you choose is what you get.

Take Collin Smith. He was fourteen years old and a three-sport athlete when a car accident broke his neck. He couldn't move from the chest down, and a wheelchair became his legs.

He chose not to let that stop him. When people ask him about it, he says, "Things in life happen. You got to let it go and move on."

He did. At age twenty-two, he graduated from High Point University.

The people to admire don't live their lives by a to-do list. They live their lives by a "to-be" list. In other words, they want to be more generous, learned, reasoned, and patient.

Those people who live by a "to-be" list have discovered wisdom…an education that serves them well for life.

FINDING YOUR PERSONAL FREEDOM

NOVEMBER 19

Sometimes you have to clear the decks of urgent matters by accepting the undesirable consequences—and then move on.

If the rent you're paying is pushing you toward your own proverbial cliff, you may need to move into less expensive accommodations until you put your financial affairs in order.

The same goes for the rest of your life. Drive a less expensive car. Eat out less often. Cut down on your entertainment budget.

These sacrifices require self-discipline, but you can muster the self-discipline—if you have created a glowing vision and can see how the sacrifices will help you reach the goals that lead toward your vision.

Harvey Dorfman once taught English and coached basketball. He later became a sports psychologist who earned World Series rings with the Oakland A's in 1989 and the Florida Marlins in 1997.

Why? He was the team's mental skills coach, who said, "Self-discipline is a form of freedom. Freedom from laziness and lethargy, freedom from expectations and demands of others, freedom from weakness and fear—and doubt."

HIT THE BULL'S-EYE
NOVEMBER 20

I f you examine the lives of great people, you'll discover that they have one thing in common: they know where they are going; they are all aiming at targets.

Stephen Hawking's classmates once called him "Einstein." At age twenty-one, he was diagnosed with amyotrophic lateral sclerosis, better known as Lou Gehrig's disease or the abbreviation ALS.

He was expected not to reach his twenty-fifth birthday. But he turned seventy-three on January 8, 2015. He never let ALS deter him from what he wanted to become—a theoretical physicist.

Hawking brought his ideas about black hole and quantum gravity to the world and spent thirty years as a full professor of mathematics at the University of Cambridge. And he did it from a wheelchair, speaking through a computer.

I have noticed even people who claim everything is predestined, and that we can do nothing to change it, look before they cross the road.

He said that from his wheelchair. And from his wheelchair, Hawking hit his target. His difficulty had nothing to do with it.

THE FACES OF INDIFFERENCE

NOVEMBER 21

M ost people would rather be treated badly than treated indifferently. Ignoring their feelings is worse than insulting them. If you really want to irritate people, be cold and unconcerned toward them.

You'll see. It's a fate worse than death. A Jewish boy from Romania believes that.

He saw it during World War II in the concentration camps where he lived. He survived, but millions of other Jews didn't. After the war, he became a writer, college professor, and an activist who went on to win the Nobel Peace Prize in 1986.

His name: Elie Wiesel. He knows what indifference looks like. Here's what he said:

The opposite of love is not hate, it's indifference. The opposite of art is not ugliness, it's indifference. The opposite of faith is not heresy, it's indifference. And the opposite of life is not death, it's indifference.

Yes, it has many faces. Don't let it be your face.

WHINING, THE OPPOSITE OF THANKSGIVING

NOVEMBER 22

At High Point University, incoming freshmen receive a clicker to use whenever they hear someone whine about something. It's a constant reminder that we are better off counting our blessings than cursing our circumstances.

Positive input must replace negative thoughts. In fact, the quickest way to cast out negative thoughts is to feed enough positive thoughts into your mind that there is no longer room for the negative ones.

When you think positively, you act positively, and you become positive.

Think what that can do.

People who take the positive view basically see the world as a good place. They actively look for the good in other people, and they act with hope and faith.

GIVING IS GRATITUDE IN ACTION

NOVEMBER 23

Think of the two seas in the Holy Land, the Sea of Galillee and the Dead Sea.

The Sea of Galilee takes in fresh water from a brook, uses it to produce a wide variety of marine vegetation life, and then gives it to the Jordan River.

In turn, the Jordan spreads the life downstream and turns the desert into a fertile plain. While the Sea of Galilee bustles with life, the Dead Sea is exactly that—a dead sea. Its water is so full of salt that it cannot sustain life.

Why? It takes in the water from the Jordan River and hangs on to it. It has no outlet.

The difference between the two seas presents a perfect picture of the differences in people. Those who get all they can tend to become self-centered and afraid that someone will steal from them.

But those who give freely of themselves usually end up having more than they can give away.

As Scottish theologian William Barclay said, "Always give without remembering, always receive without forgetting."

What a wonderful attitude to have.

BE THANKFUL

NOVEMBER 24

Imagine, for a moment, the risk the forefathers and foremothers of this country took when they crossed the Atlantic Ocean to establish their new home in America. They had no way of knowing what awaited them, no way of predicting all the hardships that would follow, no way of understanding the complexities of the challenges they would face.

They pursued with faithful courage their dream to build a better future. They planted **seeds**, worked **hard**, and when the seeds produced fruit, they gave God the glory.

They were grateful.

You, too have to take visionary and strategic risks in your life to plant seeds of greatness in your own heart and soul. Be grateful for what you have and realize that you need to contribute to what is important to you.

It could be your family, community, house of worship, or school—or something else you choose. But whatever is it, commit to contributing something and enhancing the lives of others around you. Connect, serve, and actively be thankful.

In the end, it will remind you that with God's blessing, all things are possible.

SO WHO'S INFERIOR?

NOVEMBER 25

W e all compete in a global economy, a world of 7.1 billion people—and growing—and we can't let geography and gender, accents and skin color cloud our thinking.

Financial analysts use the acronym BRICS to describe Brazil, Russia, India, China, and South Africa. These countries support about 40 percent of the world's population, and financial analysts believe by the year 2050, these BRICS nations will be the dominant force in world economics.

Albert Einstein spoke English with an accent. Indira Gandhi made her mark as a human leader, not as a female leader. And Nelson Mandela had the ability to move people with just his words.

Each example shows that accomplishments speak louder than accents, handicaps, gender, or ethnic background.

Be careful when you call someone or some country inferior. The world is changing. You need to change too.

MEEK? THINK OF MOSES
NOVEMBER 26

Some of the greatest communicators had to overcome some tough handicaps. The prophet Moses was, by his own admission, a "meek person, slow of speech." Yet he demanded that the world's mightiest ruler free the forced laborers who were making bricks for Egypt's grand building projects.

The pharaoh never listened. But 600,000 men, with their wives and families, followed Moses out of Egypt and through the parted waters of the Red Sea. And they listened when Moses, face glowing from his encounter with God, descended from Mount Sinai and gave them the Ten Commandments.

If you have a message worth delivering, deliver it with confidence and boldness. Your listeners will respect you and will be more likely to heed you if you do.

DON'T BE MISUNDERSTOOD

NOVEMBER 27

On a visit to the United States during the 1950s, Soviet leader Nikita Khrushchev held his clenched hands above his head in what appeared to be a gesture of defiance.

Those familiar with Russian culture recognized it as a gesture of friendliness, not an act of braggadocio. But the American audience that saw him on television didn't understand it that way. They got the impression of a bellicose, boorish individual.

"We will bury you!" the Soviet leader boasted.

Most Americans took it as a threat to destroy their country. The words carried a somewhat different meaning to the Russian-speaking world.

They meant this: "We will surpass you."

Khrushchev didn't intend to say that his country would destroy America. He meant only that it would surpass it economically. The lesson in all this? Remember when you're talking with people from another language or background to make sure you understand other people's intents.

No one wants to end up like Khrushchev—incredibly misunderstood.

THE KEY IS TO LISTEN

NOVEMBER 28

Listening is to hearing as speaking is to talking. Hearing is the natural response of your ears to sound. But listening is using your ears and your mind to absorb and understand what the other person is saying.

You **hear** the noise of traffic, the background music in an elevator, or the jet as it goes over your head.

But you **listen** for the sound of a ping in your engine, or to the cry of a baby to determine whether it's a cry of distress or one for attention. You **listen** when someone is giving you directions, or when people tell you what's on their minds.

Forget about your ability to think faster than another person talks. Everyone has that, but only the foolish use it.

THE POWER OF PRECISION

NOVEMBER 29

Some writers or speakers think they can hide fuzzy thinking by burying it under a mass of words. To have an impact, ideas must be expressed precisely and concisely.

Lincoln's Gettysburg Address required only 275 words, and 196 of them were of one syllable.

He didn't write it on the back of an envelope. That is simply a presidential myth. But he did mull on the speech for days before he traveled to the Pennsylvania battlefield.

He did that with all his speeches, which were short, and not laborious like the political speeches of today. They worked because they forced everyone to focus on the message they contained.

Like those 275 words, 196 with one syllable. They will never be forgotten.

Remember the importance of communicating clearly. Start today.

THERMOMETER OR THERMOSTAT?

NOVEMBER 30

A re you a thermometer or a thermostat?

A thermometer merely reflects the temperature of its environment, adjusting to the situation. But a thermostat initiates action to change the temperature of its environment.

Correspondingly, some people only adjust to their situations. They do what seems to be expected of them. They react to their environments.

Winners decide what needs to be done and take action. They drive their energies instead of being driven by them. They learn how to push things through to a successful finish and then move on to the next task.

What kind are you?

DECEMBER

YOU ARE THE DECIDER

DECEMBER 1

To make motivation pay off, you have to mobilize all of your resources in the direction of your goals. If you profess to be a positive thinker but have no aim in life, you're just spinning your wheels.

What good is all the energy in the world if you have nowhere to channel it?

Mobilizing yourself involves deciding what you want, then determining what will get you what you want.

General Colin Powell, former secretary of state and a member of High Point University's National Board of Advisors, told HPU graduates:

> We complain a lot today about politics and politicians and often for good reason. But we can't sit around waiting for superman or superwoman to come… We the people are the supermen and the superwomen. We are the deciders.

CHANGE YOUR PERCEPTION

DECEMBER 2

One salesperson in a candy store always had a line of customers waiting to be served while other sales clerks milled around with nothing to do. One day, her supervisor asked her what her secret was.

"Oh, that's simple," she replied. "The others scoop up more than a pound of candy and then start taking away. I scoop up less than a pound and add to it."

She was giving her customers a dollar's worth of value for a dollar's worth of cash. But she was leaving them with a positive perception.

And since perception is reality to the one perceiving, the customers went away happy.

So many of our actions are determined by how we perceive things to be, and how we perceive is based on what we think we hear—or see.

John Francis Bongiovi, the New Jersey son of two former Marines, said: "Miracles happen every day. Change your perception of what a miracle is, and you'll see them all around you."

Bongiovi also goes by another name: Jon Bon Jovi.

MORE THAN A FEELING

DECEMBER 3

A decision is made with the brain. A commitment is made with the heart. Therefore, a commitment is much deeper and more binding than a decision.

Commitment involves feeling as well as thinking. It is the result of a well-documented formula: thoughts plus feelings equal action.

Everything you do has to be born in the brain as an idea. That idea gives birth to a feeling. You act on the basis of the feeling. Therefore, your actions turn your thoughts into reality once you have been motivated by your feelings.

The deeper and more intense your feelings, the more powerful the motivation to turn thoughts into action.

The thought creates a vision. The feeling makes the vision glow. Action brings the vision to life.

What are you feeling today?

CHANGE YOUR WORDS, CHANGE YOUR WORLD

DECEMBER 4

In 1962, it came down to two words for President John F. Kennedy.

He had heard convincing evidence that the Soviet Union was sending ships bearing missiles and nuclear warheads for bases in Cuba, less than one hundred miles from American shores.

Kennedy thought the navy could **blockade** the Cuban coast. But that one word could have been seen as an act of war and spark a war—and possibly a nuclear conflict—between the Soviet Union and the United States.

Kennedy had declared that **no** nuclear weapons would be allowed into Cuba. What did Kennedy do? He issued a **quarantine** of Cuba to prevent any ship from bringing in military supplies.

Soviet leader Nikita Khrushchev backed down—and saved face.

"Use the right word," Mark Twain once said, "not its second cousin."

Indeed.

THINK, THE NEW ACRONYM

DECEMBER 5

Lee Colan, author of the book *Leadership Matters*, got a good piece of advice from his sister, now a high school teacher.

She shared with Colan a poster tacked up at her school. It said: Before you speak, THINK…

> T—Is it true?
> H—Is it helpful?
> I—Is it inspiring?
> N—Is it necessary?
> K—Is it kind?

We all need to avoid expressing the first thought that comes into our minds; it is not always the best thought.

It's like that verse from Proverbs: "Even fools are thought wise if they keep silent, and discerning if they hold their tongues."

That makes so much sense. Think before you speak, and you will be less likely to say something trite or offensive.

CHANGE, CHANGE, CHANGE

DECEMBER 6

You can't change other people; they have to change themselves. The only situations you can change are those relating to your own behavior, or as Gandhi supposedly once said, "Be the change you want to see in the world."

Say a good friend of yours gets obnoxious every time he drinks, and he drinks a lot. You can't force him to stop drinking. But that doesn't mean you have to put up with the consequences.

You can steer him away from where alcohol is served, encourage him to get help, or give your friend an ultimatum: get help or our friendship is over.

When you do that, you're directing your own behavior in a proactive way, and you're not assuming responsibility for someone else's behavior.

Consider this lesson from writer Maria Rodale, who wrote:

All we can really do is control what *we* decide to do. That is why we need to do what makes us feel healthy, happy, and fulfilled—do what makes us open to change. No one else can do that for us, or can make us do it, either. We can only do it for ourselves. And hopefully, by being our true, fulfilled selves we make the world a better place just by being in it.

BE YOU

DECEMBER 7

E ach of us has a personality.

It's a blending of traits, thought patterns, and mannerisms that, taken together, can aid us in communicating clearly.

Don't try to talk or write like a Harvard scholar unless you really are one.

Don't try to imitate street language unless it comes natural to you.

Be natural and let the real you come through.

Authenticity trumps charisma any day. Trust is the big thing. If you don't trust someone, you're less likely to want to be with them.

That applies to any area of life. Remember this: if you want to have a great life, enough people must say that they need you in their lives and that you bring value to their relationships.

Be authentic. Be someone other people trust. Be what bestselling author Sarah Ban Breathnach believes: "The authentic self is the soul made visible."

THE PITFALLS OF ARROGANCE

DECEMBER 8

Sooner or later, failure somehow knocks down people who become arrogant and overly proud of themselves.

Many people can take misfortune in stride and keep going. But sometimes they get spoiled by their success, and they tend to forget where they have come from and end up looking down their noses at those they feel are beneath them.

And that can lead to failure. It's one thing to be confident. It's quite another to be cocky. That reeks of conceit and arrogance.

Former Soviet leader Mikhail Gorbachev knew that firsthand. "Sometimes it's difficult to accept, to recognize one's own mistakes, but one must do it," he said. "I was guilty of overconfidence and arrogance, and I was punished for that."

We all must recognize that in ourselves. Remember 1 Samuel 2:3:

Do not keep talking so proudly or let your mouth speak such arrogance,
for the Lord is a God who knows, and by him deeds
are weighed.

Words to remember.

FINDING YOUR OWN NORMAL
DECEMBER 9

Nobody likes to work around self-centered people.

They're the people who always seem to turn the conversation toward **their** views, **their** virtues, and **their** accomplishments. Or they constantly harp on **their** aches, **their** pains, and **their** problems. They act as if they sit at the center of the universe and everything revolves around them.

Such a self-centered attitude can be self-deceiving. People who see themselves at the center of the universe often believe that everyone else thinks the way they do. This can lead them to believe that their way of thinking is the only valid way of understanding everything around them.

Such an attitude closes the door to a lot of constructive and creative ideas. Be open-minded.

Alexia LaFata is a young blogger from New Jersey who wrote:

The beauty of open-mindedness is that it allows you to find out so many new things and soak in so many new perspectives. It allows you to try on many definitions of Normal until you settle into one that feels right for you—and nobody else.

UNFOLD YOUR OWN MYTH

DECEMBER 10

People who have strong self-confidence tend to apply their personal power to useful goals. They let others talk about their abilities and deeds. They concentrate on goals, not activities. And they freely express admiration and appreciation to others.

It is enough for them to know the value of their goals and to believe in their abilities to reach them. They are far more concerned that their actions speak louder than their words.

But when they're called on it, they speak honestly. John Lennon did. He said, "If being an egomaniac means I believe in what I do and in my art or music, then in that respect you can call me that… I believe in what I do, and I'll say it."

People with self-confidence believe they can, and they do—rather than say they do.

And that has happened for centuries. Consider the thoughts of Rumi, a thirteenth-century Persian poet, who once said:

Don't be satisfied with stories, how things have gone with others. Unfold your own myth.

AN OCTAVE MADE ALL THE DIFFERENCE
DECEMBER 11

It was 1988 when George Herbert Walker Bush hired a voice coach to help him lower his voice an octave. Bush worried that his high-pitched voice had helped saddle him with an image any of us would hate. During his presidential bid, he worried his voters would see him as a weak leader.

But nothing was further from the truth. Bush already had proved his valor as a navy combat pilot during World War II.

Step back and think about it. Fairly or unfairly, we assign strength and confidence to the person who speaks with a low-pitched, well-modulated voice.

We convey specific thoughts, ideas, and information through the words we use.

But we convey feelings, moods, and attitudes through a variety of voice qualities including pitch, pace, and pause.

Bush knew that. You should too.

EDIT. EDIT. EDIT.

DECEMBER 12

Once you've spoken a sentence, you can't call it back, edit it, refine it, soften it, strengthen it, or erase it. Words that have been spoken are part of history.

But when you write a sentence, you can modify it in any way you choose. You can use Facebook, Twitter, or any social media account you have to help refine your communication skills and ultimately help anyone understand you better.

You need to remember the act of writing is really the act of thinking. It's your attempt to find meaning, solve a problem, or simply discover something about yourself—or someone else.

In writing, revision is important. Always. That is where you find the gold.

When someone praised James Michener about his writing, he corrected him: "I'm not a good writer. I'm a good **rewriter**."

He should know. Before his death in 1997, Michener wrote more than forty books, including *Tales of the South Pacific*, which won the Pulitzer Prize in 1948 and went on to become a classic Broadway musical.

YOUR CIRCUMSTANCES ARE NOT YOUR PRISON

DECEMBER 13

When you envision your future, don't limit yourself to the things you think are achievable given your present circumstances.

Without a glowing vision, you'll regard your desirable future as unattainable, and you won't focus your efforts on attaining it. You will be imprisoned by your circumstances.

As British statesman Benjamin Disraeli once said, "Man is not the creature of circumstances. Circumstances are the creatures of men."

Disraeli was prime minister twice, and he's remembered for bringing India and the Suez Canal under the control of the crown. But he also bounced back from political defeat and failed business ventures to become a prominent voice for democracy and social reform in England more than a century ago.

He truly believed a vision bypasses circumstances, and that anyone can find a way around them, over them, or under them. Or they simply can rearrange the circumstances.

Your current circumstances do not determine where you end up. They only define where you start.

BE LIKE STEAM

DECEMBER 14

People can be like water evaporating from a boiling pot and vanishing into thin air without visible accomplishment. Or they can be like steam surging through a turbine, generating power to light cities and turn the wheels of industry.

The difference is focus.

People whose lives are in focus know where they're going and have a plan for getting there. They have formed a vision of the future they desire and have set immediate, intermediate, and long-range goals for getting there.

Their actions are not haphazard.

"What do I have to do now to get to my next to goal?" they ask. Then they take action.

Goal by goal, they progress toward their desired future. Like steam through a turbine, their energy is focused on the results they are seeking.

Focus, in many ways, is more important than intelligence.

A BAD FORMULA

DECEMBER 15

If you want a formula for becoming miserable, the first rule is to think only of yourself.

People who think only of themselves—and what they want—find it hard to be happy with anything they get. For them, gaining the cooperation of others who are so vital to their success is almost impossible. Most of their personal relationships are frustrating and disappointing.

So wrap yourself around others—and what they want and need.

It's a surefire formula to eliminate misery. When you help enough people get what they want in life, they'll respond by helping you to achieve your wishes too.

LIGHTBULBS AND LASER BEAMS

DECEMBER 16

When I was a little boy, my brother gave me a small magnifying glass, and I knew immediately what its main purpose was.

When I held it at a certain distance from an object, it made it look bigger and I could see the object much more clearly. But I soon learned that it had an unsuspected power. It could focus the sun's rays on a tiny spot and, if I held it there long enough, it would burn a hole in the substance on which I focused it.

Communication works on the same principle. Focus your message on the specific audience you want, and you can concentrate and intensify your power. You will be able to gain a clearer, more thorough understanding of the people you want to reach, give them more of yourself, and bring to bear the full power of all that you have and all that you are.

Think of lightbulbs and laser beams. The only difference is focus.

YOU ARE THE PRODUCT OF YOUR CHOICES
DECEMBER 17

We can't grow by repeatedly following prescriptions. We can grow only by making new choices. We are the sum total of the choices we have made in the past.

We can change what we are in the future through the choices we make today.

Think about that.

Who do you choose to become? What do you choose to accomplish?

WATCH YOUR ATTITUDE

DECEMBER 18

Imagine starting your morning this way.

You stub your toe on the edge of the bed, get soap in your eyes in the shower, lose your contact lens in the shag carpet, spill coffee on your shirt, and leave the house without your lunch.

"It's going to be one of those days," you say to yourself.

And sure enough, your day steadily disintegrates. You arrive at work twenty minutes late, and your boss berates you with a lecture on commitment and responsibility.

The salad you buy for lunch is wilted and brown, and you can't concentrate on your work because your foot still hurts and your stomach is rumbling like Mount Saint Helens.

Not much of a day, was it? Why? What makes one day bad and another good?

Many times we can answer that question with one word: **attitude**.

You start out thinking, "Today is going to be bad." Even if something good were to happen, you'd be likely to find the negative side of it. This same principle applies to life in general.

Don't let one bad episode spoil your day or your life. Tell yourself, "That's behind me; now I'm going to enjoy what follows."

Dwelling on the negative doesn't lead to anything positive.

SIMPLE ELOQUENCE

DECEMBER 19

A speechwriter for President Franklin Roosevelt once wrote: "We are endeavoring to construct a more inclusive society."

FDR changed it to read: "We're going to make a country in which no one is left out."

There was nothing fancy in Roosevelt's words, and everyone who heard them knew exactly what he meant. The speechwriter's words were formal and pretentious.

Whomever you're communicating with, it's best to keep your language easy and informal, the kind of language people are accustomed to hearing in everyday conversation.

Persuasive communication is about clarity and brevity. It's about connecting with others in meaningful and substantive ways.

PAUL AND THE UNKNOWN GOD

DECEMBER 20

The Christian apostle Paul demonstrated an ability to establish common ground when he addressed an audience of polytheistic Greeks on Mars Hill in Athens. How was he going to persuade them to look into a religion that worshiped only one God, and an unseen one at that?

Paul began by calling attention to all the gods to which the Greeks had erected altars. Then he noted that one altar was dedicated to an unknown god. This unknown, unseen god was the one he wanted to tell them about.

Paul knew that you couldn't persuade a person to his way of thinking without beginning at their way of thinking.

He knew the Greeks believed in many gods. He realized too that they recognized the existence of an unknown god. So he started with the unknown god that they believed in and provided evidence that this unknown god was the Almighty God that he believed in.

Follow Paul's example when you're trying to persuade people to a different way of thinking.

Find some basic point upon which you can both agree and build your case from there.

CHOOSE TO BE EXTRAORDINARY
DECEMBER 21

P eople tend to live up to—or down to—your expectations of them. If you let your children know that you **expect** them to behave well in the presence of company, they're probably going to impress you.

If you expect them to behave badly, they're more likely to behave like brats. In the classroom, children whose teachers expect them to do well outperform others whose teachers expect them to fail, even though one group may be just as gifted as the other.

Our call to action at High Point University is to create an environment of excellence that commands the best of our students.

It works.

Learn to expect the best of people. Usually, they'll try to live up to your expectations. When they fall short, be forgiving.

Nobody's perfect.

YOUR TREE, YOUR SHADOW

DECEMBER 22

You can't find a more powerful medium of communication than yourself—your character, your personality, and your principles.

Our students at High Point University learn about character and begin to understand a timeless principle of life: what you value determines the principles by which you measure your behavior.

Your character, along with your personality and principles, are rooted in who you are.

Here's how Abraham Lincoln described it: "Character is like a tree and reputation like a shadow. The shadow is what we think of it; the tree is the real thing."

Another way to say it? Reputation is what people think you are; character is what God knows you are.

THE NOBLEST USE OF WEALTH

DECEMBER 23

Louis Holden, a boyish-looking university president, got the first donation Andrew Carnegie ever made to a school. In exactly four minutes, Dr. Holden collected $100,000 from a man who opened the interview by saying, "I don't believe in giving money to colleges."

How did he turn it around?

Holden did his homework. He knew that Carnegie had a deep desire to help people get started in life, and although he was the richest man of his time, he had contempt for money as a measure of success.

Carnegie once wrote: "There is no class so pitiably wretched as that which possesses money and nothing else. Money can only be the useful drudge of things immeasurably higher than itself."

Dr. Holden showed Carnegie how he could contribute to enlightenment of the mind by making a large donation to a college.

In so doing, he opened a floodgate.

By the time of his death in 1919, Carnegie had given away more than $350 million and had endowed hundreds of libraries.

Why? Carnegie believed that education was life's key and that contributing to "the enlightenment and the joys of the mind" was "the noblest possible use of wealth."

TWO WORDS, TWO MEANINGS

DECEMBER 24

One of the sad quirks of the English language is that **meekness** rhymes with **weakness**. All those poems that talk about the meekness of Jesus tend to center on that scene where He was a baby in a manger. We somehow have come to associate meekness with vulnerability and a weakness in character.

The real definition of meekness is controlled strength, and there is no better example of that than the Virgin Mary, the mother of Jesus.

For more than a thousand years, artists such as Botticelli and Michelangelo have been capturing her role as a mother and a woman. Images of her were part of an exhibit at the National Museum of Women in the Arts in Washington, DC, which featured more than sixty pieces of art created over the past five centuries, giving exhibit goers a chance to understand the beauty of art and the ultimate emblematic figure of what it means to be a believer.

There is nothing meek about that.

"I think of Mary as being brave and strong," chief curator Kathryn Wat said on National Public Radio in December 2014. "I think sometimes people see meekness and humility. I see that too but undergirding all of that I see strength."

ON CHRISTMAS...

DECEMBER 25

A s Christians, today we celebrate the birth of Jesus more than two thousand years ago in a tiny manger in Bethlehem. And as we gather with friends and family, exchange gifts, share memories, and find new traditions, we should pause to reflect on His teachings, He who is known as Immanuel.

> But I tell you, love your enemies and pray for those who persecute you, that you may be children of your Father in heaven. He causes his sun to rise on the evil and the good, and sends rain on the righteous and the unrighteous. (Matthew 5:44–45)

> A new command I give you: Love one another. As I have loved you, so you must love one another. (John 13:34)

> Here I am! I stand at the door and knock. If anyone hears my voice and opens the door, I will come in and eat with that person, and they with me. (Revelation 3:20)

In our world of 7.1 billion people, we sometimes lose sight of what's important and what we learned from a humble birth in a tiny manger.

But on Christmas we need to remember and to recall the words often attributed to John Wesley, "Do all the good you can. By all the means you can. In all the ways you can. In all the places you can. At all the times you can. To all the people you can. As long as ever you can."

Amen.

YOU'RE THE ONE WHO COUNTS

DECEMBER 26

The person who matters most is the one who stares back at you from the mirror. If your goals, and the commitment you make to them, permit you to look upon yourself with self-respect and to maintain your feeling that life is worthwhile, what does it really matter what anyone else thinks?

After all, choosing the goals on which you will spend the days allotted to you is what taking charge of your life is all about.

Literature and history are full of stories about people who allowed the opinions of others to dominate their lives, only to be disappointed with who they turned out to be.

Lift your eyes up toward the sky. Move onward and forward.

GRIND, DIG, WORK

DECEMBER 27

D are to dream! Dare to hope!

Dare to see yourself as a great big bundle of potential! Psychiatrists increasingly acknowledge the value of daydreams. Studies have shown that people who have the highest IQs tend to spend a lot of time daydreaming—imagining how things could be. Most of the truly great inventions and developments of history started out as images in the minds of dreamers.

But a dream is only a dream until you make it come true. Ralph Waldo Emerson was one of the greatest visionaries of history. In fact, many consider him the greatest mystic who ever lived. Yet Emerson wrote, "There is no way to success in our art, but to take off your coat, grind paint, and work like a digger on the railroad, all day and every day."

If it is to be, it is up to you.

CEMENT PERSONAL RELATIONSHIPS

DECEMBER 28

D oes this generation seem particularly hard on personal relationships?

The number of blended families and one-parent households is on the rise, and the traditional family is becoming increasingly rare. The American Psychological Association reports that 40 to 50 percent of married couples in the United States divorce.

The person who can negotiate the twenty-first-century obstacle course with relationships intact will hold a major psychological advantage in the race for success.

Happy couples and healthy friendships have relationships characterized by respect, affection, empathy—and commitment.

That is something legendary basketball coach Pat Riley understands. He says:

There are only two options regarding commitment. You're either in or you're out. There's no such thing as life in between.

SIX SECRETS TO SUCCESS
DECEMBER 29

All of us wonder how to make any moment special. Sometimes they just happen. But other times, we wish we had an instruction book that could give us some directions.

How? Here are some tips:

1. Accept each moment as a gift to be received with joy.
2. Use each moment to maximum productive advantage.
3. Plan for the future rather than worrying about it.
4. Learn from your mistakes; then forget them.
5. Concentrate all your energies on the task or pleasures at hand.
6. Refuse to allow the weight of an unpleasant moment or an unkind action by another person to encumber you as you move to the next moment.

PARTY ON?

DECEMBER 30

P eople who spend all their time having a ball often have nothing to go home to after the ball is over. Life can't be one continuous party. If you expect to achieve true happiness, you have to build a solid foundation for success.

That means learning new things and applying the things you learn. The occasional night on the town, the weekend vacation, and even a pressure-free day of goofing off can be refreshing and beneficial—as long as you're not goofing off on somebody else's time.

If partying and goofing off are your normal routine, you need to look for balance.

Think about that today.

Is your life balanced?

Are you achieving true happiness and building a solid foundation for success?

The answers you give will help guide your future.

RESOLUTIONS THAT COUNT
DECEMBER 31

It's New Year's Eve and time for a resolution.

Today, we believe we'll become a different person by tomorrow—or at least we'd like to think so. We'll vow to lose more weight, eat less chocolate, or not be so tied to our smartphone.

But to paraphrase *New York Times* journalist and author Hal Borland, a year's end is neither an end nor a beginning but a going on, giving us wisdom that experience can instill in all of us.

With that being said, remember:

⚙ Success does not guarantee joy. You need to add significance and fulfillment.

⚙ The truly generous don't give back. They just give.

⚙ Legacy is more important than fame and fortune.

⚙ Income is temporary; value is important.

⚙ Big things consist of little things—and you have to achieve the littlethings first.

⚙ The life worth living is one in which spiritual, mental, social, physical, intellectual, and economic dimensions are in congruence.

Happy New Year. Best of luck in your journey. Take heed of the words of Mother Teresa:

Yesterday is gone. Tomorrow has not yet come. We have only today. Let us begin.

ABOUT THE AUTHOR

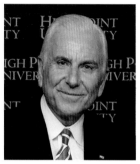

D r. Nido R. Qubein came to the United States as a teenager with limited knowledge of English and only fifty dollars in his pocket. His inspiring life story is one filled with both adversity and abundance. It is through the lens of his life's journey that one appreciates his current role as an educator, philanthropist, and passionate advocate for the development of future leaders.

Dr. Qubein has served as the seventh president of High Point University since 2005, leading the university through an extraordinary transformation that includes tripling enrollment, increasing the number of faculty from 108 to 300, and the construction of sixty new buildings on campus. Under his leadership, four academic schools have been added—Communication, Health Sciences, Art and Design, and Pharmacy. HPU's rankings moved from number seventeen to number one in Regional Colleges in the South among America's Best Colleges 2013 and 2014 by *U.S.News & World Report*. Additionally, *U.S.News & World Report* ranks HPU number one in Undergraduate Teaching in the South for 2014.

Prior to accepting his role as the president of High Point University, Dr. Qubein served as chairman of a consulting firm with clients in business and professional services. He is the recipient of many national awards, including the Cavett (known as the Oscar of professional speaking), the Horatio Alger Award for distinguished Americans, the Ellis Island Medal of Honor, the Daughters of the American Revolution's Americanism Award, and Sales and Marketing International's Ambassador of Free Enterprise. Toastmasters

International named him the Top Business and Commerce Speaker and awarded him the Golden Gavel Medal. Dr. Qubein has been inducted into the Speakers Hall of Fame and Beta Gamma Sigma, the honor society for business leadership.

He served as president of the National Speakers Association, which has a membership of four thousand professionals, and is the founder of the National Speakers Association Foundation, where the Philanthropist of the Year Award is named after him.

His business experience led him to help grow a bank in 1986, and today he serves on the board and the executive committee of BB&T, a Fortune 500 financial corporation with $230 billion in assets and 35,000 employees. Dr. Qubein is also chairman of Great Harvest Bread Company—with 224 stores in forty-two states—and serves on the board of La-Z-Boy Incorporated, one of the world's largest and most recognized furniture retailers. He also served as a former trustee of the YMCA of the USA, which oversees 2,600 YMCAs across the country.

Dr. Qubein has written a dozen books and recorded scores of audio and video learning programs. He is an active speaker and consultant addressing business and professional groups across North America. You can reach him at nqubein@highpoint.edu, or visit his website, www.nidoqubein.com.

D r. Nido R. Qubein became the seventh president of High Point University in January 2005. Since that time, President Qubein has partnered with faculty and staff to forge new opportunities for HPU. Focusing on experiential education and holistic, values-based learning, graduates are truly prepared to live a life of both success and significance. The numbers tell the story:

	2005	2015	GROWTH
Undergraduate Enrollment	1450	4300	197%
Full-Time Faculty	108	272	152%
Campus Size (Acres)	92	380	313%
Square Footage	800,000	3.4 million	359%
Buildings on Campus	22	179	714%
Total Positions	430	1400	226%
Economic Impact	$160.3 million	$464.5 million	190%
Operating Budget	$38 million	182 million	379%
United Way Giving	$38,000	$225,000	492%
Study Abroad Programs	5	41	720%

Under Dr. Qubein's leadership, HPU has delivered on its simple, yet profound promise to students and their families:

At High Point University, every student receives an extraordinary education in an inspiring environment with caring people.®

We invite you to visit and see for yourself this extraordinary place.

HIGH POINT UNIVERSITY

833 Montlieu Ave.
High Point, NC 27268
highpoint.edu
800-345-6993